THE ABINGDON WORSHIP ANNUAL 2012

CONTEMPORARY & TRADITIONAL
RESOURCES FOR WORSHIP LEADERS

The

ABINGDON
WORSHIP
ANNUAL
2012

EDITED BY MARY J. SCIFRES & B. J. BEU

Abingdon Press
Nashville

THE ABINGDON WORSHIP ANNUAL 2012
CONTEMPORARY AND TRADITIONAL RESOURCES FOR WORSHIP LEADERS

Copyright © 2011 by Abingdon Press

All rights reserved.

This book is printed on acid-free paper.

ISBN 978-1-4267-1019-3
ISSN 1545-9322

11 12 13 14 15 16 17 18 19 20—10 9 8 7 6 5 4 3 2 1

MANUFACTURED IN THE UNITED STATES OF AMERICA

CONTENTS

CONTENTS

October

November

December

CONTRIBUTORS

INDEXES

CD-ROM CONTENTS

The entire print text plus the following are found only on the enclosed CD-ROM. See the ReadMe.txt file on the CD for instructions)

CONTENTS

INTRODUCTION

As editors of *The Abingdon Worship Annual*, we speak with preachers and worship planners from a diversity of places and worship settings. In the midst of your diversity, you share a common challenge: to provide quality, integrated, creative worship week after week for congregations hungry for meaningful and fulfilling connections with God. We are honored to offer this resource as part of your journey to help your congregations grow in faith. Many of our readers also find it helpful as a weekly devotional guide or a prayer resource as they gather for lectionary study groups.

Understanding This Resource

The Abingdon Worship Annual provides ideas and suggestions for the written and spoken words of your worship services, for each Sunday (and most holy days) of the year. Each week, the ideas are centered on a theme that can be the focal point of both the preached word and the liturgy of the day. To help you plan your corporate worship services, our authors position their suggestions within a basic pattern of worship. Although you are welcome to lift an entire entry into your order of worship, feel free to mix and match in creative ways to enhance your congregation's worship experience.

Each entry includes a Call to Worship, Opening Prayer, Prayer of Confession, Words of Assurance, Response to the Word, Prayer of Thanksgiving (often considered an "Offering Prayer"), and Benediction. For those in a more casual setting, Contemporary Gathering Words or Praise Sentences are also included and can be used early in the service as a Call to Worship, or even as printed centering words for participants' reflections as they arrive for worship. Many entries also contain a litany or prayer to focus or respond to the day's message, words to call people into Passing of the Peace or to the time of Offering. Many entries also contain communion prayers and litanies. Within a communion service, you may want to insert some words for Passing the Peace. On Easter Sunday, you may choose to forego the Prayer of Confession. A Response to the Word may seem appropriate as a Benediction for your congregation. Do not feel limited by the "titles" or their placement within the service. However, simply following the order provided will offer a smooth flow to any worship service you design.

As you work with this year's resource, some comments may be helpful in making full use of its features. **Calls to Worship** are words that gather God's people together as they prepare to worship God. Often called "Greetings" or "Gathering Words," these words are typically read responsively or in unison. Some of the Contemporary Gathering Words listed in each resource may also be helpful as Calls to Worship in a traditional or blended setting. As with all responsive readings, think creatively as you plan your services. While it is simplest to have a single leader read the un-bolded words, with the congregation responding by reading the bolded words, experiment by having a pair lead in call and response format. Inviting a group of people to lead these calls can add new energy to your worship as people are surprised by the variety in leadership and format. Some congregations also enjoy responding to one another: women to men, right side to left side, children to parents. Experiment with a variety of options, and see how these words might be most meaningful in calling your congregation together to worship the Holy One.

Opening Prayers in this resource are varied in form, but typically invoke God's presence in worship. Some are more informal than others, and some are more general than formal invocations. Many can be adapted for later use in the worship service, if that suits your needs.

Prayers of Confession and Words of Assurance invite worshipers to reflect on the many ways we separate ourselves from God, and then receive God's reassurance that in Christ we are constantly reconciled back into right relationship with God. Silence also is a very powerful gift to offer during times of Confession and Assurance.

Response to the Word takes many forms in this resource. Some are in the form of a Collect (a corporate unison prayer). However, prayers need not be spoken in unison, but may be spoken alone by a single leader or led by a small group. Some of these words are in responsive form or in the form of litanies. This call and response format allows people to participate, but again can be varied in ways suggested above for Calls to Worship.

Benedictions, sometimes known as "Blessings" or "Words of Dismissal," are included in each entry. Some work best in call and response format; others seem more appropriate as a solitary blessing from the worship leader. Choose a format best suited to your congregation.

We have included a small section of opening words for worship entitled Contemporary Options to assist pastors and worship leaders in more informal or nontraditional worship settings. Those who are new to the art of leading less formal worship, sometimes called "Contemporary Worship," and those who struggle with speaking extemporaneously will find these entries particularly helpful when leading worship. Congregations unfamiliar with unison speaking in worship will find these texts simpler and more repetitive, often creating a sense of ease and comfort in informal settings. Many do not require any printed resource for full participation. Rather, leaders are encouraged to offer rote-style leadership to encourage participation. Increasingly, nontraditional congregations are utilizing screens to print responsive readings and unison prayers overhead. This may be another very helpful option for you. Both of these ideas are detailed more fully below.

Like more formal Calls to Worship, **Contemporary Gathering Words** are often read responsively. Unlike Calls to Worship, however, Contemporary Gathering Words tend to use simpler language and be more repetitive in nature. You may copy these Gathering Words onto an overhead transparency to help your congregation read responsively without being tied to a bulletin. If your congregation does not care to read words aloud, consider using two leaders to speak in call and response format. Or allow the song team or band members to act as responders to the worship leader, echoing the call and response tradition of many African American congregations.

While many of the **Praise Sentences** in this resource are easily spoken by one leader, using the call and response format is an option. In praise settings, worshipers are often willing to respond back in echo form, repeating the words or phrases spoken by the worship leader. Echoing the same words and phrases several times can be highly effective. This is a technique employed heavily in the Psalms. The Praise Sentences in this resource are not intended to limit you but rather to free you up to lead in a more informal style, where appropriate.

Included with this book are the full texts for each worship service on the enclosed CD-ROM. This will allow you to import printed prayers and responsive readings directly into your word processing program for ease of bulletin and screen preparation. Each year, we offer different additional "surprises" in the CD-ROM. This year, these bonuses include baptism liturgies, weekly song suggestions, and new worship website suggestions. We want to offer resources in ways that are most helpful, and the electronic format gives us a number of creative options that would be cost-prohibitive in print format. Please let us know what other resources would be most helpful on the CD-ROM or in the print text, as we continually strive to improve *The Abingdon*

Worship Annual to best serve the needs of local church worship leaders.

Using This Resource

As you plan worship, writing and selecting the words for worship is only one of the many tasks you must accomplish to create the beautiful tapestry of a Christian worship service. But this resource need not stand alone on your shelf. *The Abingdon Worship Annual* was written to complement *The United Methodist Music and Worship Planner* (the ecumenical version of this resource is called *Prepare! A Weekly Worship Planbook for Pastors and Musicians*), resources to guide your selection of congregational, choral, vocal, and instrumental music. Also complementing *The Abingdon Worship Annual* is *The Abingdon Preaching Annual,* with its commentaries and sermon briefs. Together, *The Abingdon Worship Annual, The United Methodist Music and Worship Planner* (or the ecumenical *Prepare!*), and *The Abingdon Preaching Annual* are a trio of resources that will be a great asset to any worship planning team.

When you are ready to design your worship service, we invite you to begin, however, not with our resource, but rather with the original text. Read through the scriptures for the day's worship service. Then read through the liturgical suggestions in this resource. Use this resource as the Spirit guides you, letting God's word flow through you and the members of your worship planning team. If an image or phrase inspires a writer on your team, take the image and run with it in your own creative ways. Trust God's guidance, and enjoy a wonderful year of worship and praise with your congregations!

Mary J. Scifres and B. J. Beu
maryscifres@gmail.com and pastorbjbeu@gmail.com

JANUARY 1, 2012

First Sunday after Christmas
Mary J. Scifres

COLOR
White

SCRIPTURE READINGS
Isaiah 61:10–62:3; Psalm 148; Galatians 4:4-7; Luke 2:22-40

THEME IDEAS
This day, which can also be celebrated as New Year's Day, is a day of both beginnings and endings. Jesus' family celebrates both an end and a beginning in today's Gospel reading. As they present Jesus to the temple, their secret Messiah-child is now revealed to temple leaders—devout Simeon and prophetess Anna. But this also begins Jesus' journey into both the Jewish community as a firstborn male and into his ministry as a specially blessed child of the temple. This "fullness of time" is not immediate but rather a journey. Likewise, our new beginnings are seldom immediate, but rather journeys into newness or new possibilities. Just as Isaiah rejoices, and all of creation is invited to praise, so we too are invited to rejoice at the new possibilities a changing calendar brings. We can praise God for the newness of Christ, born again in our lives and our world. We too are invited to grow and become strong, filled with the wisdom of God's Spirit so that God's favor may be upon us, God's own adopted children.

INVITATION AND GATHERING

Call to Worship (Isaiah 61, Isaiah 62)

Come into God's presence as a gift to God's world.
**We rejoice and celebrate, for God has clothed us
in garments of salvation.**
Do not keep silent, but sing with joy.
**We shout with praise, for God has covered us
in robes of righteousness.**
Let God's glory shine in your praise and prayer.
We will shine with the light of Christmas love!

—OR—

Call to Worship (Galatians 4)

This is the fullness of time,
the midst of the Christmas season.
**This is the fullness of time,
when we live the promise of Christmas.**
This is the fullness of time,
the cusp of a brand new year.
**This is the fullness of time,
when we live our new life in Christ.**
This is the fullness of time,
the gathering of God's worshiping children.
**This is the fullness of time.
Let us worship with joyful praise.**

Opening Prayer (Galatians 4, Luke 2)

Abba, Father God,
we come as your children
trusting in your grace.
As we come into your sacred space,
may we present ourselves
as a living gift to you
and to the needs of your world.
May our growth in your grace
strengthen our ministry as your disciples.
And may we shine forth as a beacon of hope

for all the world to see.
In Christ's name, we pray. Amen.

PROCLAMATION AND RESPONSE

Prayer of Confession (Galatians 4, Luke 2, Christmas)
Forgive us, Abba, loving Father,
when we forget the gifts of Christmas.
Break down the walls we build
that prevent your light from shining forth.
Birth in us once again
the presence of the Christ-child,
that we may be your children of grace and love.
Grow in us with the power of your Holy Spirit,
that we may become strong and wise,
resting in your favor and trusting in your grace.
In Christ's name, we pray. Amen.

Words of Assurance (Galatians 4)
You are no longer slaves, but children of God,
adopted as the children of God's very heart,
heirs of God's grace, given in Christ Jesus.
Rejoice and give thanks!
We are forgiven and made whole
in this greatest gift of all! Amen.

Passing the Peace of Christ (Luke 2, Christmas)
In peace, Christ came into our world. With peace, Christ
comes to us now. With peace, let us greet one another in
Christmas love.

Prayer of Preparation (Isaiah 61, Isaiah 62, Christmas)
Shine upon us
with the light of your wisdom, O God.
Let your salvation cover us
with righteousness and justice,
that we may shine forth like the dawn.
Let your truth and teaching
spring forth in our hearts,

3

that we may be born anew
with Christmas hope.

Response to the Word (Psalm 148)
Praise God from the heavens!
Praise God from the earth!
Praise God from the heights!
Praise God from the depths!
Praise God with the angels!
Praise God with the sun, moon, and stars!
Praise God with the mountains!
Praise God with the hills!
Praise God with the beasts!
Praise God with the birds!
Praise God forever and ever!
Praise God forever and ever!

THANKSGIVING AND COMMUNION

Invitation to the Offering (Luke 2)
From ancient times, humanity has offered gifts to honor
God and to care for God's world. Let us continue this an-
cient tradition as we receive this morning's offering.

Offering Prayer (Luke 2)
Generous God,
    receive these gifts
        as offerings of our deepest selves.
Transform them into gifts for the world,
    even as you transform us
        into children of your Spirit.
In Jesus' name, we pray. Amen.

SENDING FORTH

Benediction (Luke 2)
Let us depart in peace,
    looking for signs of salvation,
        trusting in God's word.

Let us depart in love,
    shining forth with the light of Christ.

CONTEMPORARY OPTIONS

Contemporary Gathering Words (Psalm 148, Luke 2)

Light and love, joy and hope, peace on earth,
grace for all...
    Words of Christmas stream from the heavens.
Light and love, joy and hope, peace on earth,
grace for all...
    Praises to God flow from the deep.
Light and love, joy and hope, peace on earth,
grace for all...
    **May we strengthen our world
    in word and deed.**

Praise Sentences (Psalm 148)

Sing praise to God, heaven and earth!
    We sing with the sun and the moon!
Sing praise to God, young and old!
    We sing with the shining stars!

JANUARY 6, 2012

Epiphany of the Lord
B. J. Beu

COLOR
White

EPIPHANY SCRIPTURE READINGS
Isaiah 60:1-6; Psalm 72:1-7, 10-14; Ephesians 3:1-12;
Matthew 2:1-12

THEME IDEAS
Today's scripture readings are much more than a celebration of kings bringing tribute to the Messiah. Today's readings are a promise of light to those who live in darkness; a promise of righteousness to those who suffer at the hands of others; a promise of grace to those who are lost; and a promise of salvation to the Gentiles. Epiphany is a day to celebrate God's love for all—especially those who are most in need of God's light and love.

INVITATION AND GATHERING

Call to Worship (Isaiah 60, Psalm 72)
Arise, shine, for your light has come.
   The glory of the Lord bathes us
   in the brightness of the dawn.
Lift up your eyes and look around.

**Our hearts rejoice in the glory of God's Son,
who defends the cause of the poor,
delivers the needy, and crushes the oppressor.**
Christ is like rain that falls on mown grass,
like showers that water the earth.
**Let us bring him sweet-smelling gifts
and pearls from the sea.
Let us offer him hearts full of praise.**
Arise, shine, for your light has come.
The glory of the Lord shines upon us.

Opening Prayer (Isaiah 60, Psalm 72, Ephesians 3, Matthew 2)
God of starlight,
    disperse the darkness of our lives,
        that we may behold the light of your love
            shining in every corner of our world.
Guide our footsteps in the paths of righteousness,
        that justice may flourish and peace may abound.
Help us follow the kings of old,
        that through our own journeys of faith,
    we may behold the mystery made known
            through the coming of your glory
                in the infant Jesus. Amen.

PROCLAMATION AND RESPONSE

Prayer of Confession (Matthew 2)
Eternal God,
    we celebrate the courage of kings
        who left their homelands and their own people
            to follow a star;
    we marvel at their quest to honor a child
        whose power was announced
            in the heavens above;
    we would do anything to be part of their story—
        as long as it requires little effort
            or sacrifice on our part.

1

Forgive our feet of clay, O God.
Open our shut-up hearts
    to the mystery made known in Christ,
    that others may behold in us,
        the blessings to be found
            in journeys worth taking. Amen.

Assurance of Pardon (Ephesians 3)
The power of the living God
    transforms our hearts of stone
    into hearts that sing with gladness.
The power of the living Christ
    brings light and salvation
    to those who turn to God.

Response to the Word (Psalm 72, Ephesians 3)
The word of God is stronger than the foundation
of the earth.
    Let those who oppress the poor tremble.
The word of God brings righteousness.
    Let the sinner repent and return to the Lord.
The word of God shines the light of salvation
into the darkness of our lives.
    Let all those who love God shout for joy.

THANKSGIVING AND COMMUNION

Offering Prayer (Psalm 72)
Merciful God,
    may your justice roll down like waters,
    your righteousness like an ever-flowing stream.
May these gifts and offerings
    be an answer to your call—
        a call to deliver the needy,
        rescue the weary,
        and hearken to the voice
            of the poor and the helpless,
Bless these signs of our love for you, O God,
    as we proclaim your glory to the nations. Amen.

SENDING FORTH

Benediction (Isaiah 60, Psalm 72)

Follow the kings of old and search for God's Son.
We go forth, following the light of the world.
Follow the magi in search of the child of peace.
**We go forth, proclaiming hope and blessing
to the poor and needy.**
Follow the star to behold the glory of God.
We go with the promise of new life in Christ.

CONTEMPORARY OPTIONS

Contemporary Gathering Words (Isaiah 60, Matthew 2)

Look up and see the star.
Is that God's light shining in the darkness?
Look around and see the star child
in the one sitting next to you.
**Is that the light of Christ I see
in the eyes looking back at me?**
Look inside yourself and see Christ's light within.
Is the light of the Spirit everywhere?
Everywhere. Come worship the light of the world.

Praise Sentences (Matthew 2)

Christ is our light!
Shine with the brightness of the star child.
Christ is our king!
Bring him gifts of gold, frankincense, and myrrh.
Christ is our life!
Offer him gifts of love and joy.
Christ is in our midst!
Praise him with music and worship.

JANUARY 8, 2012

Baptism of the Lord
Mary Petrina Boyd

COLOR
White

SCRIPTURE READINGS
Genesis 1:1-5; Psalm 29; Acts 19:1-7; Mark 1:4-11

THEME IDEAS
This is a day of beginnings. In the beginning, God created the universe and proclaimed it good. At the beginning of Jesus' ministry, God proclaimed that this was the beloved Son. The Spirit sweeps across the waters, bringing the world into being; the Spirit descended on Jesus, bringing blessing to the beginning of his ministry; the Spirit came upon those early disciples, filling the church with strength and power.

INVITATION AND GATHERING

Call to Worship (Genesis 1, Mark 1)
In the beginning, God created the heavens
and the earth.
  God said, "Let there be light!"
There was evening and there was morning.
  God called it good.

Jesus came up from the waters of the Jordan.
God said, "You are my Son, the Beloved."
There was for us a new beginning.
God called it good.
We gather here to praise the God of blessing.
This is a day of new beginnings!

Opening Prayer (Genesis 1, Acts 1, Mark 1)
Creating Spirit,
as you called the world into being,
call us together as your church.
Give us power and strength to serve the world.
Give us wisdom to see the goodness in creation.
Blessing Spirit,
as you named Jesus the Beloved,
name us and bless us with your grace,
that we, your children, may tell your story.
Empowering Spirit,
fill the church with your strength,
that it may carry your love
throughout the world. Amen.

—OR—

Opening Prayer (Genesis 1, Acts 1, Mark 1)
God who creates,
the wind of your Spirit swept across the waters,
and the world was there.
God who calls,
your Spirit spoke at the waters of the Jordan
naming Jesus as your child.
God who blesses,
you gave us your Spirit
in the waters of our baptism,
naming us as your children
and giving us an unquenchable thirst
for your glory.
May the waters of your grace
flow through our lives,
and become a river of righteousness. Amen.

11

PROCLAMATION AND RESPONSE

Prayer of Confession (Genesis 1, Acts 1, Mark 1)
Creating God,
 you formed the world and called it good.
Yet, we take our earth for granted:
 consuming its resources,
 polluting its air and water,
 ignoring its beauty.
You called forth humanity and called it good,
 yet we treat one another with disrespect:
  ignoring those in pain,
  choosing violence over peace.
We repent of the many ways
 we have dishonored your gifts.
We turn our lives toward you,
 opening ourselves to the power
  of your transforming love.
Shine the light of your grace upon us,
 that we may see your way.
Send your Spirit upon us,
 giving us the power to proclaim your word. Amen.

Words of Assurance (Genesis 1, Mark 1)
The breath of God
 sweeps across the waters of your life,
 recreating you, forgiving you,
 calling you good.
You are God's beloved child,
 forgiven and made whole through the Spirit.

Passing the Peace of Christ (Psalm 29, Acts 19, Mark 1)
Our God of power and might gives the people peace.
Christ, the beloved, embodies peace. The winds of the
Spirit bring us peace. With this same spirit, share signs of
peace with one another.

Response to the Word (Genesis 1, Mark 1)
Creating God,
 you brought forth the world,

ordering its days,
illuminating our lives.
May the light of your love shine upon us,
that we may live as your beloved children.
May the power of your Spirit
transform us into witnesses of your love. Amen.

THANKSGIVING AND COMMUNION

Invitation to the Offering (Genesis 1, Mark 1)
God creates all that is and calls it good. From the goodness of God's world, let us bring our gifts, that all the people may live in peace as God's beloved children.

Offering Prayer (Genesis 1, Mark 1)
Spirit of power and strength,
    you called forth the world
        and pronounced it good.
Spirit of life and love,
    you sent Jesus to bless the world.
Accept these gifts,
    that they may continue your work,
        creating a just world
            where all your beloved children
                may live in peace.

Great Thanksgiving (Genesis 1, Mark 1)
Praise to you, almighty God,
    creator of the universe.
By your breath the world came into being.
At your word light broke forth,
    banishing the darkness.
You brought order out of chaos.
Night follows day;
    morning light emerges from the darkness.
You created all that is and called it good.
And so, we your people join all creation
    as we praise you, God of glory and strength.
(Sanctus)

13

You sent John the Baptist into the wilderness,
 proclaiming forgiveness and preparing the way
 for the one who would baptize with the Spirit.
Jesus was baptized by John,
 and as the Spirit descended, your voice proclaimed,
 "You are my son, the beloved;
 with you I am well pleased."
Jesus taught your ways of love and forgiveness.
He healed the world's brokenness.
He proclaimed your vision of justice
 and righteousness for all.

At a meal with friends, he broke bread, gave thanks,
 and shared it with them, saying,
 "This is my body, offered for you."
Then he took the cup. Again he gave thanks
 and shared it with those gathered together:
 "This is the cup of the new covenant,
 a sign of my life, offered for forgiveness.
 Do this and remember."
And so we do this,
 partaking of bread and wine as the body of Christ,
 remembering his life,
 offering ourselves in your service
 as we proclaim the mysterious depth of your love.
(Memorial Acclamation)

Send the breath of your love upon those gathered here,
 that we may become the body of Christ.
Send the winds of your Spirit
 upon these elements of bread and wine,
 recreating them into the living presence
 of Jesus Christ.
Unite us at this table, that we may serve the world.
All majesty, glory, and strength is yours,
 Creator, Word, and Spirit. Amen.

SENDING FORTH

Benediction (Psalm 29)
> The God of glory and strength sends us forth to serve.
> **We have seen the splendor of God.**
> The voice of God is powerful, giving us power.
> **We have heard the voice of God.**
> May the Lord give us strength!
> **May our God bless us with peace.**

CONTEMPORARY OPTIONS

Contemporary Gathering Words (Genesis 1, Mark 1)
> In the beginning, God created!
> **God created the world.**
> In the beginning, God created!
> **God created the light.**
> In the beginning, God blessed!
> **God blessed the beloved Son.**
> In the beginning, God blessed!
> **God blesses us today!**

—OR—

Contemporary Gathering Words (Genesis 1)
> In the beginning—
> **God**
> In the beginning—
> **Creation**
> In the beginning—
> **Light**
> In the beginning—
> **Love**
> In every beginning—
> **Praise the God of light and love!**

Praise Sentences (Psalm 29)
> The voice of God is strong, shaking the earth.
> The Spirit of God is powerful, fulfilling our lives.
> Praise the God of power and strength!

JANUARY 15, 2012

Second Sunday after the Epiphany
Mary J. Scifres

COLOR
Green

SCRIPTURE READINGS
1 Samuel 3:1-10 (11-20); Psalm 139:1-6, 13-18;
1 Corinthians 6:12-20; John 1:43-51

THEME IDEAS
If ever there was a day to explore our embodiment, today
is the day. As incarnate beings like Samuel (1 Samuel 3:11)
and Nathanael (John 1:48-49), we can hear and see God in
action. We can listen and observe like Eli (1 Samuel 3:8)
and Philip (John 1:43-45), alerting others to the Spirit's
presence. As embodied spirits, we are called to glorify
God, even in the use of our bodies. In all these things, God
searches and finds us, knows our physical choices as well
as our spiritual paths. Spirit and body are not separate but
intertwined, mutually called into this ministry for those
who have heard, "Follow me," and yearn to respond,
"Here I am."

INVITATION AND GATHERING
Call to Worship (1 Samuel 3)
Listen in the stillness of the morning,

in the hush of this moment.
Listen for the Spirit of God . . .

Call to Worship (1 Samuel 3, Psalm 139, John 1)
(This may be used alone or following the previous Call to Worship after a moment of silence.)
God searches to find you and calls you by name.
Speak, O God, for your servant is listening.
God hems you in and lays the hand of blessing
upon you.
Here I am, Lord, willing to serve.
Christ calls to you now: "Follow me."
Here I am, Lord. Lead on!

Opening Prayer (1 Samuel 3, Psalm 139, John 1)
Wonderful God of all knowledge,
    share your wisdom with us
        in this time of quiet reflection.
Open our ears to hear your call.
Widen our vision to see your presence.
Broaden our thoughts to know your ways.
Speak to us now.
In hope and trust, we pray. Amen.

PROCLAMATION AND RESPONSE

Prayer of Confession (1 Samuel 3, Psalm 139, John 1)
O God,
    you have searched us and known us.
When we are following you with confidence
    and when we are hiding out of fear,
        you are with us.
Your knowledge is too wonderful for us,
    and yet it is your knowledge
        that we so desperately need.
Speak to us now.
Reveal our sins,
    that we may truly repent and repair the damage
        we have wrought upon others.

Cover our shame
    with the robe of your love and acceptance.
Empower us with the wisdom of your ways.
Strengthen our courage and commitment
    to follow you in service to others.
In Christ's name, we pray. Amen.

Words of Assurance (Psalm 139, 1 Corinthians 6)
God has formed our very being,
    making even our bodies members of Christ.
We are united to God in Christ's love and grace.
Celebrate God's forgiveness for you and for me!
You are now one spirit with God!

Passing the Peace of Christ (John 1)
Christ's presence in one another brings us peace. Let us
share signs of this peace and hope together as we pass the
peace of Christ.

Response to the Word or Benediction (1 Samuel 3, Psalm 139, 1 Corinthians 6, John 1)
The God who searches and knows us
calls us by name.
    God speaks in the hope that we are listening.
Forming us and shaping us for service,
the Spirit blesses us with gifts.
    Our bodies, minds, and spirits
    are temples of blessing,
    a gift of trust from God's Holy Spirit.
Come and see. Follow and serve.
Christ sends us to do great things.
    Here I am. Send me, even me.

THANKSGIVING AND COMMUNION

Invitation to the Offering (1 Samuel 3, Psalm 139, 1 Corinthians 6, John 1)
Paul reminds us, "Your body is a temple of the Holy Spirit
within you." The Spirit speaks, "Come and see." Christ
calls, "Follow me." We, who are fearfully and wonderfully

made, are entrusted to listen and respond with generosity
and love.

Offering Prayer (1 Samuel 3, Psalm 139, John 1)
God of seeing and knowing,
> thank you for seeing so many possibilities
> > within us.
Use our gifts and offerings
> to transform possibilities into realities,
> that others may come and see your grace.
Speak through us and through these gifts,
> that others may hear and respond
> > as you call them by name.

SENDING FORTH

Benediction (1 Samuel 3, Psalm 139, John 1)
Even at the end, God is with us.
> **Even as God has spoken, God is still speaking.**
Go forth—listening and seeing, learning and growing.
> **We go forth in God's grace, following Christ,**
> **ready to serve the world.**

CONTEMPORARY OPTIONS

Contemporary Gathering Words (1 Samuel 3, John 1)
Listen for the word of God.
> **But God's word is rare these days!**
Seek God's truth in all of life.
> **But God's truth is hard to find!**
Come and see, look for Christ's presence.
> **But Christ's presence is difficult to see!**
In ancient times and recent days, we may doubt God,
but God does not doubt us.
> **God's word is always here,**
> **ever ancient, ever new.**
Come and see, listen and learn.
> **God is speaking to all of us now.**

Praise Sentences (1 Samuel 3, Psalm 139, John 1)
Praise God who knows us so well!
Praise God who knows us so well!
Praise God who calls us by name!
Praise God who calls us by name!

JANUARY 22, 2012

Third Sunday after the Epiphany
Peter Bankson

COLOR
Green

SCRIPTURE READINGS
Jonah 3:1-5, 10; Psalm 62:5-12; 1 Corinthians 7:29-31;
Mark 1:14-20

THEME IDEAS
God's call is clear: "Follow me!" When we are awake to
God's call, we can be led into surprising, unconventional
places; we can even turn away from what our culture labels
truth. With the realm of God close at hand, the Holy One invites us to be part of the solution. The call is clear and ur-
gent: We are to be ready to turn to this new, unexpected Way.

INVITATION AND GATHERING

Call to Worship (Psalm 62)
The God of all creation calls us.
   **We come, knowing that our deliverance
   and honor rest in God.**
Power and steadfast love belong to God.
   **We come to sing and pray,
   celebrating the presence
   of this mighty, loving God.**

Opening Prayer (Jonah 3, 1 Corinthians 7)

Holy One, God of all Creation,
 you call us to be your people,
  to carry your vision in this time and place,
  to go where you send us
  to help welcome your amazing good news.
As we gather in the presence of the risen Christ
 to spread the news that your realm is near,
  fill us with your Holy Spirit,
  O God of all Creation.
Fill us with your glorious Spirit,
 that we may share your good news
  with a world in need.
Amen.

PROCLAMATION AND RESPONSE

Prayer of Confession (Jonah 3)

Holy Fountain of Forgiveness,
 the tale of Jonah reminds us
  of your never-ending love for all creation.
May we be like the people of Nineveh,
 who were able to acknowledge their sin
  and open their eyes to your healing presence.
Though you stand ready to forgive our sin,
 we find it easier to bite our tongues,
  clench our fists,
   and cling to our hurts and resentments
    rather than let you open our hearts.
We trust you, Holy One;
 we pour out our hearts to you.
Receive the pain that lurks in our humanity,
 as we offer up what we have hidden
  from ourselves and from the world—
   those words and deeds
    that keep us separated from your love.

Words of Assurance (Psalm 62)
When we repent, our God relents,
lifting us beyond the pain, restoring us to safety,
protecting us in the refuge of eternal love.
In the name of Jesus, who is the Christ,
you are forgiven.
In the name of Christ, you are forgiven.
Glory to God. **Amen.**

Passing the Peace of Christ (Mark 1)
Jesus calls us to repent and draw near to him, to share the
realm of God and the peace that passes all understanding.
May the peace of Christ be with you always.
May the peace of Christ be with you always.

Prayer of Preparation (Jonah 3, Psalm 62, Mark 1)
Holy God, creator of a new reality
    just now coming into view,
    we have come today to see and touch
        and know your presence here among us.
Be with us as we listen for your call.
Help us hear afresh the good news:
that power and steadfast love
    arise from you, our rock and our salvation. **Amen.**

Response to the Word (Jonah 3, Mark 1)
God of new realities close at hand,
    open our ears to hear your call.
Give us the insight to know that it is you who calls us.
Grant us the courage to go where you send us
    as we journey with the risen Christ. **Amen.**

THANKSGIVING AND COMMUNION

Invitation to the Offering (Mark 1)
Our nets are full enough to share God's bounty. Our
hearts are open wide to the needs of others. Let us reach
out and share what we've been given.

Offering Prayer (Jonah 3, Mark 1)
Holy God, Steadfast Rock of all Salvation,
we marvel at the strength of your compassion
and your ability to offer forgiveness.
We come to you,
hungry to be part of the good news
you are bringing forth,
for we would be part of the realm
you are revealing. Amen.

Invitation to Communion (Psalm 62)
Holy God, we thank you for your steadfast love
that shelters and protects us.
You are our rock and our salvation.
Loving Christ, we yearn for, yet dread,
to hear your invitation: "Follow Me!"
**You call us to risk everything
to help you bring good news to the world.**
Empowering Holy Spirit, we give thanks
that you fill our lives with joy.
**Fill us now as we gather to share your presence
in the bread and cup. Amen.**

SENDING FORTH

Benediction (Jonah 3, Psalm 62)
As we go out to meet a changing world,
remember this: God alone is our rock
and our salvation; the risen Christ
is calling each of us to share the good news
of the realm of God.
**The realm of God is near,
and we are on the way. Amen.**

CONTEMPORARY OPTIONS

Contemporary Gathering Words (Psalm 62)
Where do I turn for help?
God is my rock. I will not be shaken!

24

Where do I look for forgiveness?
God is my salvation. I will not be shaken!
Where can I find protection?
God is my fortress. I will not be shaken!
Trust in God, our refuge and our hope.

—OR—

Contemporary Gathering Words (1 Corinthians 7, Jonah 3, Mark 1)

The present form of this world is passing away.
The realm of God is near.
When Jonah spoke, the people woke
and changed their ways.
Repent! God will relent!
When Jesus called, they left their nets
and followed him.
The realm of God is near. Repent!
God will relent!

Praise Sentences (Jonah 3, Psalm 62)

Praise the God of all Creation.
Worship the One who calls us—
speaking with a different voice,
offering an unexpected invitation.
Celebrate the presence of our loving God.
Rejoice, the realm of God is near.

JANUARY 29, 2012

Fourth Sunday after the Epiphany

B. J. Beu

COLOR

Green

SCRIPTURE READINGS

Deuteronomy 18:15-20; Psalm 111; 1 Corinthians 8:1-13;
Mark 1:21-28

THEME IDEAS

In today's readings, the mighty acts of God are inter-
woven with the promise to teach God's people the ways
of life. God is awesome and worthy to be praised, but also
to be feared. In Deuteronomy, the people are so frightened
by the immediacy of God's power that they seek guidance
through intermediaries, prophets, lest they come in direct
contact with the holy and die. The psalmist proclaims
God's faithfulness not only for our physical needs but for
our spiritual needs as well. The fullness of God again ap-
pears to the people in Christ, who heals and teaches with
authority.

INVITATION AND GATHERING

Call to Worship (Psalm 111, Mark 1)
    Listen, Christ is teaching.
    We sit at the feet of our teacher.

Watch, Christ is setting the captives free.
In him we see the power of God.
Rejoice, Christ is in this very room.
We gather in awe and wonder.

—OR—

Call to Worship (Psalm 111)
Praise the Lord!
We praise God with full hearts.
Fear the Lord!
Fear of the Lord is the beginning of wisdom.
Delight in the Lord!
**We delight in God's works
and rejoice in God, our savior.**
Praise the Lord!
We praise God with full hearts.

Opening Prayer (Mark 1)
God of power and might,
when your awesome presence
was too much for your people to bear,
you sent prophets to guide,
to teach, and to call us back
to the ways of life.
In the fullness of time,
you again dwelt powerfully with your people,
sending your Son Jesus
to open our eyes,
that we might see your ways anew;
to open our hearts and minds,
that we might understand
and proclaim your teachings
for all to hear. Amen.

PROCLAMATION AND RESPONSE

Prayer of Confession (Deuteronomy 18)
Mighty God,
we love to hear your deeds
of power and might,
imagining that we would not tremble with fear,
if we saw you before us in a pillar of fire
or column of smoke.
But as we wander lost in our own wilderness,
we know only too well our own fear and dread
of being in your awesome presence.
Send us prophets to teach us your ways.
Help us recognize them within our midst,
that we might hear your words
in the lessons they teach. Amen.

Words of Assurance (Psalm 111)
The psalmist knew that fear of the Lord
is the beginning of wisdom,
but also that God is gracious and merciful.
Rejoice in the knowledge that our heritage
is established by the One who is faithful.
Thanks be to God!

Response to the Word (Deuteronomy 18)
Where have all the prophets gone?
They are all around us,
here in our midst.
What have they to teach us?
They teach us God's ways,
as they have of old.
In whose name do they speak?
They speak in Christ's name,
and in the name of God.
How will we know if they speak the truth?
The Spirit will testify to the truth,
as it has always been.

THANKSGIVING AND COMMUNION

Offering Prayer (Deuteronomy 18, Psalm 111)
God of splendor and might,
    you lead us across the wilderness of our lives,
        setting our hearts aflame;
    you teach us the ways of life and death
    and send us prophets to bless us
        with new understanding and wisdom.
May these offerings be a sign
    of our thankfulness and our commitment
        to grow ever deeper in your ways,
        through the one who leads us into life. Amen.

SENDING FORTH

Benediction (Psalm 111)
The works of the Lord sustain us.
God has blessed us with life.
The precepts of the Lord guide us.
God has blessed us with wisdom.
The love of the Lord redeems us.
God has blessed us with salvation.
Go with God's blessings.

CONTEMPORARY OPTIONS

Contemporary Gathering Words (Psalm 111)
What are you waiting for?
Praise the Lord, laugh, and sing.
We'll shout God's praises for all to hear!
Stop daydreaming.
Listen to the Lord, learn, and live.
We'll hear God's word
and ponder anew the mysteries of God.
Let's get going and really worship.
Our God is an awesome God,
greatly to be praised!

Praise Sentences (Psalm 111)
Praise the Lord!
Delight in God's works!
Praise the Lord!
Rejoice in God's word!
Praise the Lord!
Praise the Lord!
Praise the Lord!

FEBRUARY 5, 2012

Fifth Sunday after the Epiphany
Mary J. Scifres

COLOR
Green

SCRIPTURE READINGS
Isaiah 40:21-31; Psalm 147:1-11, 20c; 1 Corinthians 9:16-23;
Mark 1:29-39

THEME IDEAS
God's awesome power binds all of these scriptures together, but especially the readings from Isaiah and Psalm
147. In 1 Corinthians and Mark, Paul and Jesus utilize the
power of God to perform mighty acts and proclaim the
message of God's powerful love. God's power is seen
beautifully in creation, as Isaiah points out. This power is
a comfort God offers to us, reminding us of God's ability
to give power to us in our weakness and healing to us in
our illness. This mighty power is most miraculously seen
in Christ's acts of healing and casting out demons.

INVITATION AND GATHERING
Call to Worship (Isaiah 40)
Have you not known? Have you not heard?
Has it not been told from the beginning of time,
    in the voice of the wind
    and the splendor of the sky?

31

Our Creator God is from everlasting to everlasting.
(This can also lead into the responsive Call to Worship or Contemporary Gathering Words below.)

Call to Worship (Isaiah 40)

Lift up your eyes to the witness of the earth.
God's presence is here,
in the plants and the trees.
Lift up your eyes to the canvas of the heavens.
God's praises are proclaimed by the stars above.
Lift up your eyes to the love of God.
God's grace abounds,
in the courage of the weak
and the strength of the downtrodden.
Lift up your voices to join in the song.
It is good to sing praise to our Creator God!

Opening Prayer (Isaiah 40)

Everlasting God,
how good and fitting it is
to sing your praises and worship your name.
From the beginning of time,
you have revealed yourself to us
in mighty acts of power
and miraculous gifts of grace.
From the tiniest seed to the mightiest ocean,
you show us your presence and your power.
Speak to us now,
that we may truly hear.
Inspire us now,
that we may truly know.
Lift up our eyes,
that we may truly see
you as the everlasting God,
the One who never faints or grows weary.
Lift up our hearts,
that we may truly feel your strength
at every moment of our journey. Amen.

PROCLAMATION AND RESPONSE

Prayer of Confession (Isaiah 40, Psalm 147, Mark 1)
God of grace and glory,
    we come to you in our human frailty.
We come faint with exhaustion.
We come downtrodden with powerlessness.
We come embarrassed by our sinfulness.
We come sick with fever or burdened with sorrows.
Bind up our wounds, O God.
Heal our broken hearts.
Forgive our mistaken actions.
Release our destructive thoughts.
Lift us up,
    that we may walk in your light,
    forgiven and free, strengthened and renewed,
        to be the delight of your eyes.
In hope and gratitude, we pray. Amen.

Words of Assurance (Isaiah 40, Mark 1)
Have you not known? Have you not heard?
Has it not been told to you
from the beginning of time?
The everlasting God, Creator of earth and sky,
    is the God of grace and glory,
    embracing us with forgiveness and mercy,
    strengthening us with hope and courage.
Lift up your eyes and see.
God's love abounds in power!

Passing the Peace of Christ (Mark 1)
Lifted up, freed and forgiven, we are invited to serve one another in grace and peace. Let us share signs of servanthood and love, as we greet one another with the peace of Christ.

Response to the Word or Prayer of Preparation (Isaiah 40)
Everlasting God,
    we listen, expectant,
        and you speak wisdom and truth;

THE ABINGDON WORSHIP ANNUAL 2012

we wait, exhausted,
    and you lift us up;
we run, with perseverance,
    and you lead the way;
we walk, unsure,
    and you hold our hands.
Your understanding is unsearchable,
    your grace immeasurable.
Guide us in our search
    and strengthen us on our journey.
Embrace us as your children,
    sending us forth to proclaim the news
        of your loving power
            to all the ends of the earth.

THANKSGIVING AND COMMUNION

Invitation to the Offering (Isaiah 40, Mark 1)
Like Jesus before us, let us go beyond our own communities to proclaim the message of God's loving power and
grace. Let us share what we have, that people throughout
the world may hear and know of God's everlasting love.

Offering Prayer (Isaiah 40, Psalm 147)
May these gifts of money and ministry
    be like wings to the exhausted
        and strength to the powerless.
May these gifts of ours
    bind up the brokenhearted
    and welcome the outcast.
And may our offerings of time, talent, and treasure
    sing your praises and be a cause of delight
        throughout your marvelous world.

The Great Thanksgiving (Isaiah 40)
The Lord be with you.
And also with you.
Lift up your hearts.
We lift them up to the Lord.

Let us give thanks to the Lord our God.
It is right to give our thanks and praise.
It is right, and a good and joyful thing,
always and everywhere to give thanks to you,
almighty God, creator of heaven and earth.
From everlasting to everlasting,
you have revealed your mighty presence to us.
Have we not known? Have we not heard?
From the beginning,
you have created and are creating.
When we have not known or heard,
when we have forgotten or neglected your truth,
you have redeemed us and renewed us.
From the earth's first gardens to mountaintop storms,
you have spoken to us and entrusted us
to be your people.
From laws on tablets to warnings from prophets,
you have spoken your truth
and renewed your covenant with us.
And so, with your people on earth,
and all the company of heaven,
we praise your name
and join their unending hymn, saying:
Holy, holy, holy Lord, God of power and might,
heaven and earth are full of your glory.
Hosanna in the highest! Blessed is the one
who comes in the name of the Lord.
Hosanna in the highest!

Holy are you and blessed is your holy name.
In the fullness of time, you sent your Son, Jesus Christ
to reveal your powerful love in the world.
Healing and teaching, proclaiming and prophesying,
Christ continues to reveal your presence
even now.
Through Christ's powerful love and endless grace,
we are invited into your presence,

rescued from our sins, and led on your path
of justice and righteousness.
In Christ's grace, we renew our strength
and rise up with wings like eagles.
As children of your new covenant,
sealed by water the Spirit, we come to you now
with joy and gratitude,
remembering how Jesus shared bread and wine,
even when he faced weakness and fear,
and shared it with friends and betrayers,
disciples and deniers alike.

On that night before his death, Jesus took bread,
gave thanks to you, broke the bread,
gave it to the disciples, and said,
"Take, eat; this is my body which is given for you.
Do this in remembrance of me."
When the supper was over, Jesus took the cup,
gave thanks to you, gave it to the disciples,
and said, "Drink from this, all of you;
this is my life in the new covenant,
poured out for you and for many
for the forgiveness of sins.
Do this, as often as you drink it,
in remembrance of me."
And so, in remembrance of these
your mighty acts of love and grace,
we offer ourselves in praise and thanksgiving,
as children of your covenant,
in union with Christ's love for us,
as we proclaim the mystery of faith.
Christ has died.
Christ is risen.
Christ will come again.

Communion Prayer (Isaiah 40)
Pour out your Holy Spirit on all of us gathered here
and on these gifts of bread and wine.

Make them be for us the life and love of Christ,
    that we may be for the world the body of Christ,
    redeemed and renewed by his love and grace.
By your Spirit, lift us up with wings like eagles,
    that we may know the strength
    to truly become one with Christ,
    one with each other,
    and one in ministry to all the world
    until Christ comes in final victory,
    and we feast at the heavenly banquet.
Through Jesus Christ, with the Holy Spirit
    in your holy Church, all honor and glory is yours,
    almighty God, now and forevermore. **Amen.**

Giving the Bread and Cup
*(The bread and wine are given to the people, with these or other
words of blessing.)*
The life of Christ, living in you.
The love of Christ, flowing through you.

SENDING FORTH

Benediction (Isaiah 40, Mark 1)
Renewed and strengthened,
let us go forth with faith and hope.
    Lifted by God, renewed by Christ,
    we go to be signs of love and grace.

CONTEMPORARY OPTIONS

Contemporary Gathering Words (Isaiah 40, Psalm 147)
Lift up your eyes and see.
    Our God is an awesome God.
God is from everlasting to everlasting.
    Our God is an awesome God.
Hear the song of the earth
and the praise of God's people.
    Our God is an awesome God.

Come, let us worship with joy
the God who is awesome enough
to strengthen us in our weakest days
and lift us up from our deepest sorrows.
Our God is an awesome God!

Praise Sentences (Isaiah 40, Psalm 147)

Sing praise to God, who is gracious and good.
Sing praise to the God of love.
Hope in the Lord, who is faithful and true.
Sing praise to the God of love.
Trust in our God, who strengthens us all.
Sing praise to the God of love.

FEBRUARY 12, 2012

Sixth Sunday after the Epiphany
Matthew J. Packer

COLOR

Green

SCRIPTURE READINGS

2 Kings 5:1-14; Psalm 30; 1 Corinthians 9:24-27; Mark 1:40-45

THEME IDEAS

Healing and restoration unite these passages. Second Kings and the Gospel lesson offer very different accounts of lepers receiving healing. Naman is an army commander in high favor with king Aram. He comes to Elisha in power and arrogance and almost goes away uncleansed. Contrast this with the leper in the Gospel, who comes in humility, kneeling before Jesus and begging for healing. Both, in the end, are healed because of their faith—in Naaman's case, the faith to perform the required actions; in the case of the leper in Mark, by his faith alone. Psalm 30 also speaks of deliverance and restoration. Although they run their "race" in different ways (see 1 Corinthians), both lepers receive the "prize."

INVITATION AND GATHERING

Call to Worship (Psalm 30)
I will extol you, O Lord, for you have drawn me up,
and did not let my foes rejoice over me.

O Lord my God, I cried to you for help,
and you have healed me.
Sing praises to the Lord, faithful ones,
and give thanks to God's holy name.
God's anger lasts for a moment,
but God's favor is for a lifetime.
You have turned my mourning into dancing.
You have taken off my sackcloth
and clothed me with joy.
Weeping may linger for the night,
but joy comes with the morning!
O Lord my God, I will give thanks to you forever.
My soul praises you. I will not be silent.

Opening Prayer (Psalm 30)
Holy One,
you turn our mourning into dancing.
Speak to us in silence,
in words and in actions,
that as we gather today to praise you,
we may hear your voice.
Transform us, we pray,
in the name of your Son, Jesus Christ,
and through the power of the Holy Spirit. Amen.

PROCLAMATION AND RESPONSE

Prayer of Confession (2 Kings 5, 1 Corinthians 9, Mark 1)
Healing God,
we come to you this day
confident in your power
to renew and restore our lives.
There are times we come to ask for healing,
but our pride stops us
from accepting what you offer.
There are times when we run strong and confident,
infused by your grace and mercy.

But there are times when our faith falters,
   and we lose the strength and hope within us.
O God,
   forgive us when we fall short of the finish line
      because we chose to rely upon our own power.
Forgive our unwillingness to accept your divine touch.
If you choose, Lord, you can make us clean. Amen.

Words of Assurance (Mark 1:41, 1 Corinthians 9)
Hear these words from the Lord:
   "I do choose. Be made clean!"
Arise in God's power.
Run strong and confident once again.

Passing the Peace of Christ
As a healed and forgiven people of God, greet one another
with the peace of Christ.

Introduction to the Word or Prayer of Preparation
Open our minds to truth that teaches.
Open our hearts to truth that touches.
Open our lives to truth that transforms.
Amen.

Response to the Word (Psalm 30)
Gracious God,
   our souls praise you and cannot be silent.
Lord, Our God,
   we give thanks to you forever. Amen.

THANKSGIVING AND COMMUNION

Invitation to the Offering
The act of giving is more than a Christian obligation, it
is a joyful response to the love of God. Whatever we give
of our time, our talent, and our treasure, we offer back
to God what was God's to begin with, and what God
chose to share with us. Freely you have received. And so,
freely give.

Offering Prayer (Psalm 30)
> Giving God,
>> we sing praises to you
>>> and give thanks to your holy name.
>> Thank you for this opportunity
>>> to share all that we have
>>> and all that we are.
>> Use these offerings
>>> so others will know of your abundant love
>>>> freely offered through your Son, Jesus Christ. Amen.

SENDING FORTH

Benediction (Mark 1)
> Cleansed and transformed by the love of God,
>> go into the world to spread the good news.
> Share God's blessings with all you encounter
>> through the power of the Spirit dwelling in you.
> Go and be a living witness to the healing power
>> of our Lord. Amen.

CONTEMPORARY OPTIONS

Contemporary Gathering Words (Psalm 30)
> Sing praise to the Lord and give thanks
>> to God's holy name.
> God's anger is but for a moment
>> while God's favor lasts a lifetime.
> Weeping may linger for the night,
>> but joy comes with the morning!

—OR—

Contemporary Gathering Words (Psalm 30:11-12)
> Give thanks to the Lord, our healer.
>> **God has turned our mourning into dancing!**
> Give thanks to the Lord, our restorer.
>> **God has turned our mourning into dancing!**

Give thanks to the Lord, our transformer.
God has turned our mourning into dancing!
Come, let us worship the Lord!
Let us praise and not be silent.
Let us give thanks forever!

Praise Sentences (Psalm 30:1-3)
I will extol you, O Lord, for you have drawn me up.
O Lord, my God, I cried to you for help,
and you have healed me.
O Lord, you brought up my soul
and restored me to life.

FEBRUARY 19, 2012

Transfiguration Sunday
Laura Jaquith Bartlett

COLOR
White

SCRIPTURE READINGS
2 Kings 2:1-12; Psalm 50:1-6; 2 Corinthians 4:3-6;
Mark 9:2-9

THEME IDEAS
The temptation with the Transfiguration story is to over-analyze it. The same can be said about the story of Elijah's departure. There are so many strange and bizarre details that it is easy to get sidetracked trying to make sense of it all. But the elements of blazing light and intense glory seem to indicate that the mystery itself is part of the gift of the story. God cannot be explained, but even more amazing is the fact that God has invited us *into* the light. Will we have the courage to accept the invitation?

INVITATION AND GATHERING
Call to Worship (Psalm 50)
God speaks and the earth is created.
   Glory hallelujah!
God shines forth with a beauty
beyond our comprehension.

Glory hallelujah!
God calls us to be a people of faith.
Glory hallelujah!

Opening Prayer (2 Kings 2, Psalm 50, 2 Corinthians 4)
God of glory and wonder,
    you call us to come live
        in the radiance of your love.
We acknowledge our utter inability
    to understand the scope of your being.
At times we simply stand in awe and amazement.
But you summon us to be your faithful people
    as you shine your love into our hearts.
Give us the courage to pick up the mantle of hope.
Help us move forward,
    following the light of Christ,
        this and every day. Amen.

PROCLAMATION AND RESPONSE

Prayer of Confession (2 Corinthians 4, Mark 9)
For the times we choose the veil of darkness
over your gospel of light,
    forgive us, Lord.
For the times we choose to proclaim ourselves
instead of proclaiming Jesus Christ,
    forgive us, Lord.
For the times we choose mindless action
over heartfelt devotion,
    forgive us, Lord.
For the times we choose the bonds of fear
over the freedom of your grace,
    forgive us, Lord.

Words of Assurance (2 Corinthians 4)
God said, "Let light shine out of darkness."
This same God shines in our hearts
    to give us the light we see in the face
    of Jesus Christ.

45

Leave the darkness behind,
and accept God's invitation to live in the light.

Passing the Peace of Christ

The light of Christ shines forth in this place today! Let us remind one another of the joy that is available when we choose to step out of the darkness. Turn to those around you and offer these simple words, "God invites you to live in the light!"

Response to the Word (Mark 9)

(Ideally, this would be read slowly by two contrasting voices. It can be used as a responsive reading for two groups, or for the leader with the entire congregation responding.)
On the mountaintop:
fresh air, lightshine.
Gathered with the prophets:
holy time, lightshine.
Listening to God's voice:
identity revealed, lightshine.
In the company of Jesus:
awesome wonder, lightshine.
Coming down the mountain:
tearful reflection, lightshine.
Back to reality:
transfigured lives, lightshine.
(2-3 seconds of silence, then both voices):
Lightshine!

THANKSGIVING AND COMMUNION

Offering Prayer (Mark 9)

Awesome God,
confronted by the dazzling light of your glory,
we want to stay on the mountaintop
and worship you.
But you call us to do more than worship,
you call us into action as your disciples.

Through these gifts,
    may we shine the transforming light of your love
    into all the world.
Use our worship, use our gifts, use our lives,
    in the name of Jesus Christ. Amen.

SENDING FORTH

Benediction (2 Kings 2, Mark 9)
    Leave this place today
        dazzled by the glory of our amazing God.
    Go down from the mountain
        to live in the light of Jesus Christ,
        God's own beloved Son.
    May the fire of the Holy Spirit
        blaze a transforming path into the world
        where you are called to serve. Amen.

CONTEMPORARY OPTIONS

Contemporary Gathering Words (2 Kings 2, Mark 9)
    It's a steep climb up the mountain.
    God gives us strength for the ascent.
    The light is shining on the mountain.
    God opens our eyes to holy splendor.
    We don't know what to do on the mountain.
    God provides a guide and companions.
    We are ready to come out of the darkness.
    God calls us to live in the light!

Praise Sentences (2 Corinthians 4)
    Come see the glory of God!
    Come proclaim Jesus Christ as Lord!
    Come live in the light!

FEBRUARY 22, 2012

Ash Wednesday
Sara Dunning Lambert

COLOR
Purple

SCRIPTURE READINGS
Joel 2:1-2, 12-17; Psalm 51:1-17; 2 Corinthians 5:20b–6:10; Matthew 6:1-6, 16-21

THEME IDEAS
Ash Wednesday is about redemption, preparation, and cleansing from sin. The Joel passage reminds us that the day of the Lord is coming, so we must return to God, whose steadfast love will sanctify and bless the generations. This theme of repentance also carries through the other scripture lessons. "Create in me a clean heart" (v. 10), cries the psalmist, for a spirit ready for purification is necessary for reconciliation with God. In the passage from 2 Corinthians, redemption and deliverance are emphasized as keys to faith. Matthew prepares us to pray with humility, seeking only the treasure we store in heaven. God's mercy and grace flow through these scriptures, leading toward the hope of salvation by faith, with the promise of Christ's love.

INVITATION AND GATHERING

Call to Worship (Joel, Psalm 51, 2 Corinthians 5–6, Matthew 6)
The day of the Lord is coming.
Let us prepare for the promise of redemption.
We come to the altar to pray.
Despite impending dark and gloom,
the message is clear: God's steadfast love
spills light into all corners of the earth.
We come to the altar to weep.
Return to the Lord with all your energy and passion,
for God's mercy and grace abound.
We come to the altar to receive.
We lay our imperfections at your feet, O Lord,
watching and waiting in faith.
We come to the altar to listen.
Fashion within us a new joy, O God,
as we await deliverance from hopelessness, sin, and fear.
We come to the altar to rejoice. Amen.

—OR—

Call to Worship (Joel 2:12, Psalm 51, 2 Corinthians 5–6)
Gather the people.
Darkness has spread over the land.
Sound the alarm, the day of the Lord is near!
God beckons:
"Return to me with all your heart."
Sustain in me a willing spirit.
Have mercy according to your steadfast love.
Create in me a clean heart.
Today is the day of salvation!

PROCLAMATION AND RESPONSE

Prayer of Confession (Psalm 51, 2 Corinthians 5–6, Matthew 6)
Holy God,
we come to you with willing spirits

and open hearts,
yet our frail nature often betrays us.
We delight in feeling your love—
your compassionate arms surround and protect us,
despite the many obstacles
we place in your way.
As our expectant hearts stir with hope,
we lean on your forgiveness to wash us,
guide us, and defend us from harm.
In this time of searching,
bless our efforts to gather treasure fit for heaven.
Help us dispel the darkness within,
and conquer our fears
as we join the pilgrimage toward your grace.
In Christ's name we pray. Amen.

Words of Assurance (Joel 2:12, 2 Corinthians 5–6, Matthew 6)
"Yet even now," says the LORD,
"return to me with all your heart."
We ask for mercy, and find it waiting
before the request is even made.
Be assured, therefore, that you are blessed
and purified in God's name.

Passing the Peace of Christ or Benediction
May the peace of Christ bless your journey into Lent.
**May the peace of Christ bring forgiveness
to your life.**
May the peace of Christ go with you today
and always.
And also with you.
Now is the time, today is the day!
Amen.

Introduction to the Word or Prayer of Preparation (Psalm 51)
Great Redeemer,
we come with receptive minds, pliant hearts,

and willing spirits to hear your scripture,
grasp your message,
and comprehend your love.
As we contemplate the meaning
of palm branches turned to ash,
may we understand your healing power
that cleanses our souls and prepares us
for your promise of faith renewed.

Response to the Word (Joel 2, Psalm 51, Matthew 6)
Holy One,
give us wisdom in our secret hearts
to hear and understand your word.
As we journey through Lent,
we rest in your steadfast love—
a love that bears us toward the promise
of resurrection.
By the example of your disciples,
we travel in faith together
toward the glory of Christ.

Invitation to Imposition of Ashes (Joel, 2 Corinthians 5–6, Matthew 6)
Blow the trumpet in Zion and assemble the congregation as we tremble in anticipation. The day of the Lord is near! We come ready to listen, watch, and wait. We come prepared to cleanse our souls and purge our spirits of all impurities. The time is right and the time is now. May the ashes of our lives bring healing within as we receive these ashes upon our foreheads. We ask for God's blessing, God's ever-present love and mercy, as we receive the sign of our willingness to walk with Christ all the way to the cross. Amen.

THANKSGIVING AND COMMUNION

Offering Prayer (Joel 2, Psalm 51, Matthew 6)
All that we have comes from you,
Creator and Sustainer.

May these symbols of your gifts
> bring light to a dark and treacherous world,
> just as your truth brings joy and gladness to all.
Receive our earthly treasure,
> given freely for your good work
> > in humanity's name. Amen.

Invitation to Communion
We stand at your table
> to weep, fast, mourn, and pray, O Lord.
The ashes of your grace
> mark us for your salvation.
In the breaking of the bread,
> and the pouring of the cup,
> we realize once again
> > the awesome power of your love for us.
The sins of our past rinsed clean,
> we remember the sacrifice of your Son.

Let all come who are sincerely penitent and seek the love of
God, through Christ the Son. The table is open. No obstacle
stands in the way of you who truly search for truth and faith.

SENDING FORTH

Benediction (Psalm 51, 2 Corinthians 5–6, Matthew 6)
May the steadfast love of God
> sustain you in the weeks ahead,
> as you discover again the power of prayer.
Treasure God's grace and seek joy in redemption,
> giving thanks for the tasting of your souls.
For now is the time, today is the day of salvation!

CONTEMPORARY OPTIONS

Contemporary Gathering Words (Joel 2, Psalm 51, 2 Corinthians 5–6)
We gather the faithful in love and peace,
> seeking the acceptable time of salvation.

As our hearts and minds are cleansed and purified
  by God's merciful grace,
    we will truly know the power of redemption.
Bless and purify the generations
    with the mark of holy ashes,
      so all may know that we love Christ.

Praise Sentences (Joel 2, 2 Corinthians 5–6, Matthew 6)
  Now is the time, today is the day of salvation!
  While treasure on earth soon fades,
    our cherished faith remains!
  Blow the trumpet in Zion,
    for the day of the Lord is near!
  The palms of joy
    have become the ashes of redemption!
  O Lord, open our lips,
    and our mouths will declare your praise!

FEBRUARY 26, 2012

First Sunday in Lent

Ken Burton

COLOR

Purple

SCRIPTURE READINGS

Genesis 9:8-17; Psalm 25:1-10; 1 Peter 3:18-22; Mark 1:9-15

THEME IDEAS

With the sign of the rainbow, God enters into a covenantal relationship with humanity. The psalmist sings of the Holy One's steadfast love and faithfulness within the covenant. At his baptism, Jesus is proclaimed as God's beloved Son, issuing in a new covenant of loving faithfulness through our baptism by water and the Spirit.

INVITATION AND GATHERING

Call to Worship (Psalm 25, Mark 1)
To you, O Lord, I lift up my soul.
In you, O God, I place my trust.
Make known your paths.
Lead me in your truth.
Your kingdom is coming near.
Be present in our midst.
To you, O Lord, I lift up my soul.
In you, O God, I place my trust.

Opening Prayer (Genesis 9, Psalm 25, Mark 1)
Faithful Maker of Rainbows,
 your loving presence is with us now,
  even as it was with Noah
   in the days of the flood,
  and continued with Jesus
   through his trials in the wilderness.
Make your paths known to us,
 that we may walk in your ways
 and abide in your truth.
For it is you who holds our hearts,
 it is for you that we wait. Amen.

PROCLAMATION AND RESPONSE

Prayer of Confession (Mark 1, Genesis 9)
Holy One, we often lack the courage and strength
 to resist the temptations in our path.
It is so hard to believe that your realm is near,
 so hard to act as if we truly believe.
We fail to hear your call in our lives,
 we miss your rainbow among the clouds.
 Hear us now as we confess our weaknesses
  and temptations.
(A time of silence may follow.)

Words of Assurance (Mark 1, Psalm 25)
Our Creator God sustains us in paths of love
 and faithfulness.
Jesus the Christ offers us repentance and new life.
The Holy Spirit breathes fresh energy
 and strength through us.
The God who calls us "beloved"
 offers us forgiveness of sin and fullness of grace.

Response to the Word (Genesis 9, Psalm 25)
Holy One,
 we have seen your rainbow of promise
 and have heard your word of hope.

Be with us now
as we respond with renewed courage and power.
May we truly be your people!
Amen.

THANKSGIVING AND COMMUNION

Invitation to the Offering (Mark 1)
The time is fulfilled, and the realm of God has come near.
Let us be generous with our offerings.

Offering Prayer (Mark 1)
Receive these offerings, O God.
May they be for us gifts of love.
**Use them as you will,
for in giving, our lives find fulfillment.**

SENDING FORTH

Benediction (Mark 1)
As you sent Jesus forth from the wilderness
to proclaim your realm, so send us forth now
to love and serve a broken world.
Amen.

CONTEMPORARY OPTIONS

Contemporary Gathering Words (Psalm 25)
Teach us your paths.
Let us know your ways.

—OR—

Contemporary Gathering Words (Genesis 9)
We see the rainbow in the sky,
and know God's love will never end.
We see the rainbow in the heart,
and know Christ's grace will never fail.
We see the rainbow in the soul,
and know the Spirit's life will never die.

Praise Sentences (Genesis 9, Psalm 25)
> Your colors fill the sky, O God.
> Your rainbows lighten our day.
> All praise to you who brings us hope.
> All praise to you who fills our lives with joy.
> Your colors fill the sky, O God.
> Your rainbows lighten our day.
> (B. J. Beu)

MARCH 4, 2012

Second Sunday in Lent
Mary J. Scifres

COLOR
Purple

SCRIPTURE READINGS
Genesis 17:1-7, 15-16; Psalm 22:23-31; Romans 4:13-25;
Mark 8:31-38

THEME IDEAS
Naming, covenant, and faith journeys emerge themati-
cally in all of today's scriptures. As covenant people, we
take on new names: Abram becomes Abraham; Sarai becomes Sarah; fisherman Simon becomes disciple Peter;
spouses often take the same last name; adopted children
are given a family "surname"; the baptized proclaim their
name as their "Christian name"; newly converted people
proudly label themselves "Christian." These new names
are symbolic of new journeys, proclamations of faith, and
promises of covenantal relationship. As we reflect on
names that change and names that remain steadfast, we
are invited to reflect on our journeys of faith. For faith remains steadfast as a foundation upon which we can grow,
even as faith changes with us, transforming us and calling
us forth to new journeys and challenges.

INVITATION AND GATHERING

Call to Worship (Genesis 17, Romans 4, Mark 8)

From generation to generation, God calls to us.
Christ names us as God's own people.
In hope and faith, God walks before us.
Christ calls us to pick up our cross and follow.
In covenant and love, God promises us grace.
Christ carries us forward into life anew.

Opening Prayer (Genesis 17)

God of Abram and Sarai,
  you call to us across the span of time.
Open our minds,
  that we may discern your call,
  even as you name us anew.
Grant us hope against hope,
  that we may trust your guidance
  and walk in your ways.
Raise us up to newness of life,
  that we may be children of your promise,
  people of your covenant,
  and disciples who follow your every lead.

PROCLAMATION AND RESPONSE

Prayer of Confession (Genesis 17, Psalm 22, Romans 4, Mark 8)

God of grace and glory,
  forgive us when our failed faith
  causes us to stumble or stop
  on this journey with Christ.
Grace us with faith that hopes against all hope,
  so that we may trust in your promises
  and walk in your ways.
Lift us up,
  that we may carry our cross
  and continue on the path to new life.

Words of Assurance (Genesis 17, Romans 4, Mark 8)
Like Abram and Sarai before us,
  we have been claimed as God's own.
Like Simon and Levi,
  we have been named by Christ
  as chosen disciples.
Through Christ, our faith has been reckoned
  as righteousness.
In Christ, we are forgiven
  and raised to new life.
My friends, we are forgiven and loved by God!

Passing the Peace of Christ (Mark 8)
Let all who would become Christ's followers deny themselves and follow Christ in love and grace, even when the
burden is heavy and the road is long. Let us love, as Christ
would have us love, as we turn to our neighbor with signs
of grace and peace.

Prayer of Preparation or Response to the Word (Genesis 17, Mark 8)
O Promised One,
  you come to us with ancient truths
    and new insights.
Let the ageless message of faith
  be our foundation.
Let the ever-changing experience of grace
  be our strength.
Guide us to be your covenant people—
  to follow as you call us forth,
    that we may be a blessing to all the nations
    and a light of love for all to see.

THANKSGIVING AND COMMUNION

Invitation to the Offering (Genesis 17, Mark 8)
As sisters and brothers with Christ in God's holy
covenant, we are called to be fruitful and foundational in
strength and love for all the peoples of this earth. Let our

time of offering challenge us to carry the cross of love, bearing burdens for those who cannot bear their own burdens, showing grace to those who know only shame, and offering hope to those who are haunted by hopelessness. As we deny ourselves and our instincts for self-protection, we become Christ-like in our giving and in our loving. And in losing our hold on the world, we gain a foothold on the journey toward God's eternal love.

Offering Prayer (Genesis 17, Psalm 22)
Bless us and our gifts this day,
    that we may be a blessing
        to all the ends of the earth.
As these gifts go forth into the world,
    may the ministries they support
        help others remember and turn to you, O God,
        recognizing the great love and grace
            you shower upon us all.

Great Thanksgiving (Genesis 17, Lent)
Lift up your hearts!
    We lift them up to God!
Celebrate God's love!
    It is right to give God our thanks and praise!
We give thanks and praise to you,
    our Guide and Guardian!
We celebrate your creative presence
    that has called forth this glorious earth
    and the heavens above.
We praise and glorify you
    for creating us in your very image.
We celebrate the long history
    when you traveled with us,
    guiding us along the way.
From the days of ancient covenants—
    on the journey with Abram and Sarai,
    to their children and great grandchildren—
    you continue to speak and name us as your own.

Speaking through the prophets,
    you called us back into covenant,
    that we might be people of justice
    and righteousness.
(Sanctus may be added here.)

In the fullness of time, you came to us
    in the presence of Jesus the Christ,
    showing us the way of strength and trust.
Even when faced with impending death,
    Christ gave thanks and blessed the fruit
    of this, your good earth,
    offering not only bread and wine,
    but the bread of life and the wine of salvation.
We remember his prophetic words:
    "Take, eat, this is my body, broken for you.
    Take, drink. This is my life poured out for you
    and for many."
As we walk this journey of life,
    we remember these gifts
    as we proclaim the mystery of faith.
    Christ has died.
    Christ is risen.
    Christ will come again.

Prayer of Consecration (Genesis 17)
    God of grace and glory,
        send your Holy Spirit upon us
            and upon these gifts of bread and wine.
    Name us as your own.
    Lay claim on our lives
        and upon these gifts,
        that we may be your people
            and these gifts may be sustaining grace
                for the journey of faith.
    In Christ's name we pray. Amen.

SENDING FORTH

Benediction (Genesis 17, Mark 8)

Christ has named you. God has claimed you.
The Spirit sends you forth.
We go where the Spirit leads—
to the ends of the earth,
to the streets of our town,
to the homes of those in need.
Go forth to be a blessing, followers of Christ,
children of the covenant.
We go to share hope against hope,
grace upon grace, the love of God
flowing through us.
Go in peace, for God is with you
both now and forevermore.

CONTEMPORARY OPTIONS

Contemporary Gathering Words (Genesis 17, Psalm 22, Romans 4, Mark 8)

Names, places, promises, dreams...
memories that shape our lives.
Hear God calling: You are named Christ's children.
See this place: God is present all around.
Know the promise: Christ is with us always.
Share the dream: Hoping against hope,
we have found grace and love.
May the dream and the truth of God's love
flow to the ends of the earth.

Praise Sentences (Psalm 22)

Praise our God! Glorify God's holy name!
Praise our God! Glorify God's holy name!
Standing in awe, we worship the God of love!
Standing in awe, we worship the God of love!

MARCH 11, 2012

Third Sunday in Lent
Laura Jaquith Bartlett

COLOR
Purple

SCRIPTURE READINGS
Exodus 20:1-17; Psalm 19; 1 Corinthians 1:18-25; John 2:13-22

THEME IDEAS
The theme of God's covenant is woven throughout these Sundays in Lent. The commandments of Exodus 20 must be understood in the context of the promises made to Noah (Lent 1) and to Abraham (Lent 2). These are not so much nit-picking prohibitions as they are descriptions of what it means to live in covenant with the God of grace. And in John's Gospel, we begin to understand that God's ultimate promise has been made flesh in Jesus Christ, whose life and death and resurrection heal all the brokenness of the world.

INVITATION AND GATHERING

Call to Worship (Psalm 19, Exodus 20)
The heavens are telling the glory of God.
   The word of God is a living promise!
The law of the Lord is perfect.
   The word of God is a living promise!

The covenant of God shall last forever.
The word of God is a living promise!

Opening Prayer (Psalm 19, Exodus 20)

(Before the prayer, announce that there will be opportunities to share from our experience.)
Awesome God,
   we have come together
      to join with creation
         in proclaiming your glory.
All around us are examples
   of your power and majesty
      which we lift up to you now...
(Allow time for sharing.)
And all around us are examples
   of your abiding love and grace,
      which we confess with our lips...
(Allow time for sharing.)
We pray this day for the strength and courage
   to enter faithfully into your covenant,
      opening our hearts, our souls,
      our lives in grateful praise.
Thank you for the gift and example
   of your Son Jesus Christ,
      in whose name we pray. Amen.

PROCLAMATION AND RESPONSE

Prayer of Confession (Exodus 20)

God of the Covenant,
   we thank you for the promises
      you have made and kept with us
         through the ages.
The strength of your love binds us together
   in spite of our many shortcomings.
You make clear the expectations for your children
   in the commandments you handed down
      to your servant Moses.

And yet, too often we treat those laws
  as if they were a menu to pick and choose from
  as it suits us.
Though we hope never to kill another person,
  we do not think twice about breaking the Sabbath,
  or wonder how to truly keep it holy.
We do not bow down to gold statues,
  but we do pledge our allegiance to idols:
    money, work, sports, prestige, ego, politics,
    even TV shows.
God, bring us back into true covenant with you.
Through your grace, remind us yet again
  that your love for us has never wavered.
(Prayer continues in silence.)

Words of Assurance (Psalm 19)
God's promises are true and unbroken.
God's grace is sweet and abundant.
God's word is perfect and life giving.
Come, enter into the joy of God's forgiving love!

Prayer of Preparation (Psalm 19)
Prepare us now to hear your holy scriptures, O God.
Enable us to revel in the sweetness of your words.
Help us delight in the perfection of your laws.
Revive our souls
  with the wisdom of your commandments.
Empower our voices
  to join with the heavens
    as we proclaim your glory. Amen.

Response to the Word (Genesis 9, John 2)
God, we are afraid of earthquakes, tsunamis, floods.
Show us a sign!
God has set a rainbow in the clouds.
God, we are afraid that we have lost our identity
in the fast-moving world of the twenty-first century.
Show us a sign!

God has made us all descendants of Abraham,
children of the promise, heirs of salvation.
God, we are afraid of losing those we love the most.
Show us a sign!
God has triumphed over even death.
Through Christ's resurrection,
all our fears are banished!

THANKSGIVING AND COMMUNION

Invitation to the Offering (John 2)
In our zeal to kick the money changers out of the temple, we sometimes feel that money itself has no place in the church. We forget that we can use our dollars to do amazing things in the name of Jesus Christ. Here in this place, at this very moment, we have the opportunity to share our gifts—including our financial resources—to become full participants in God's promise of love and justice for everyone. Come, participate in God's promise through your gifts and offerings.

Offering Prayer
Faithful God,
    we give you thanks for the constancy
        of your promises through all generations.
We offer these gifts
    as willing partners in your covenant.
Guide us to use these resources
    as we work toward the fulfillment of your promise
        to bring about your kingdom on earth.
In the name of Jesus,
    who is your living promise to all humanity, amen.

SENDING FORTH

Benediction (Exodus 20, Psalm 19, John 2)
Go now as partners in God's covenant.
Know that the constancy of God's law will guide you,
    the grace of Jesus Christ will sustain you,
        and the daring of the Holy Spirit will empower you
        to live in the glory and joy of God's promises. Amen.

CONTEMPORARY OPTIONS

Contemporary Gathering Words (Exodus 20, John 2)
Broken promises, empty dreams, shattered hearts...
God's covenant remains strong.
Broken laws, weak faith, rampant doubts...
God's covenant remains strong.
Broken systems, financial corruption,
unfettered greed . . .
God's covenant remains strong.
In the midst of a broken world,
we come to worship as God's own people,
trusting the unbroken promise of eternal love and life!

Praise Sentences (Psalm 19)
The heavens are telling the glory of God!
All of creation witnesses to God's creative power.
The laws of God sustain and uphold us.
The commandments of God are sweeter than honey.
Let us worship and rejoice!

MARCH 18, 2012

Fourth Sunday in Lent / One Great Hour of Sharing

Mary J. Scifres

COLOR

Purple

SCRIPTURE READINGS

Numbers 21:4-9; Psalm 107:1-3, 17-22; Ephesians 2:1-10; John 3:14-21

THEME IDEAS

God's grace is not only the focus of Lent, but of today's scriptures in particular. The mercy of a bronze serpent gives the Israelites salvation from the poisonous serpents biting at their heels. How much greater is the mercy shown to us through Christ's presence in our lives! Give thanks for this amazing grace and steadfast love indeed!

INVITATION AND GATHERING

Call to Worship (Ephesians 2, John 3)

Give thanks and sing of mercy and grace!
We sing of God's amazing love.
Rejoice and offer praise, for Christ is here.
We worship the one who lives.
Walk in the light; live in this love.
**Redeemed and reclaimed,
we live in the Spirit of love.**

Opening Prayer (Ephesians 2, John 3)
Good and gracious One,
    we cry out and you hear our voice.
You lift us up with your love
    and offer us the light of your grace.
Let the richness of your mercy flow through our lives,
    that we may worship you in spirit and truth.
May we go forth as children of light and love,
    in the name of Christ,
        in whom we find hope. Amen.

PROCLAMATION AND RESPONSE

Prayer of Confession (Psalm 107, Ephesians 2, John 3)
Merciful God,
    hear the cries of our hearts.
Forgive the sickness of our sin
    that would lead us to death and despair.
Raise us up to new life,
    that we might taste of eternity
        as we walk in the light
            of your love and grace.

Words of Assurance (Psalm 107, Ephesians 2, John 3)
God did not send Jesus to condemn the world,
    but rather that we might know salvation and grace
        through Christ.
Behold the steadfast love that endures forever!
In this love we are forgiven and redeemed by God.

Passing the Peace of Christ (Psalm 107, Ephesians 2)
Let the redeemed proclaim God's steadfast love. Proclaim
Christ's love to one another with signs of forgiveness and
grace. Let us pass the peace together.

Response to the Word (Psalm 107)
Gathered as God's people, let us reflect on the ways in
which God gathers the scattered fragments of our broken
lives to offer healing and hope.
(A time of silent reflection may follow.)

Prayer of Response (Ephesians 2, John 3)
Rich in mercy and abounding in great love,
God has given us life in Christ.
Raise us up even now, O God,
that we may be signs of hope for all to see.
Immeasurable grace and unending kindness
are the gifts we are freely given.
Live as light in our lives, O Christ Jesus,
that we may be light and love for the world.
We are the children of God:
created for goodness, prepared for grace.
May we walk in God's ways
and love as Christ loved,
that all may know the goodness of God!

THANKSGIVING AND COMMUNION

Invitation to the Offering (Psalm 107, Ephesians 2)
Let us offer thanksgiving sacrifices and signs of grace
through our gifts to God this day.

Offering Prayer (Ephesians 2, John 3)
God of steadfast love and never-ending grace,
thank you for the gifts of eternity entrusted to us—
gifts of love and grace,
that others may know hope and joy.
Bless these gifts we return to you now,
that they may be a taste of eternity
and a promise of new life
through the ministries of this church.
In Christ's name, we pray. Amen.

Invitation to Communion (Numbers 21, Ephesians 2)
This is the table of grace.
In Holy Communion,
manna in the wilderness becomes the bread of life
for all who call upon the name of Christ.
In Holy Communion,

the law of the Lord becomes the law of love.
In Holy Communion,
    the promise of eternity comes to us
    as mercy and grace,
    that we might know God
    in the breaking of the bread
    and the sharing of the cup.
Come to the table of grace.
Taste of the promise of God.
Feed on the law of love,
    and your cup will be filled with living water
    that never ends.

SENDING FORTH

Benediction (Ephesians 2, John 3)
Light has come to our world!
We go forth as light for the world.
Love has come to our lives.
We go forth as love for the world.
Grace and mercy is ours.
We go forth as givers of grace and peace!

CONTEMPORARY OPTIONS

Contemporary Gathering Words (Numbers 21, Ephesians 2, John 3)
We who are dying are promised life.
We who are wandering in darkness are offered light.
Come to the One who offers mercy and grace,
    that we may worship in the light of God's love!

Praise Sentences (Psalm 107, Ephesians 2)
Give thanks to our God, for God is good!
God's love endures forever!
Sing with the earth:
 from east and west, north and south!
God's love endures forever!
Tell of Christ's deeds of amazing grace!
God's love endures forever!

MARCH 25, 2012

Fifth Sunday in Lent
B. J. Beu

COLOR

Purple

SCRIPTURE READINGS

Jeremiah 31:31-34; Psalm 51:1-12; Hebrews 5:5-10;
John 12:20-33

THEME IDEAS

God is always seeking our renewal. The prophet Jeremiah
proclaims that the days are coming when God will make
a new covenant with Israel—a covenant written on the
heart. The psalmist proclaims that we will be washed
clean by God and have a new spirit placed within us.
Jesus proclaims that such renewal requires sacrifice, even
death—for unless a grain of wheat dies, it yields no fruit.
The author of Hebrews maintains that Christ has made
the sacrifice necessary for this renewal in our lives.

INVITATION AND GATHERING

Call to Worship (Jeremiah 31, Psalm 51:10-12)
God is here to wash away all defilement;
cry out with the psalmist:
  "Create in me a clean heart, O God,
   and put a new and right spirit within me."

Christ is here to lead us back to the ways of life;
call out your petition:
> **"Cast me not away from your presence,**
> **and take not your Holy Spirit from me."**

The Spirit is here to renew and revive our souls;
reach for God with all your strength:
> **"Restore to me the joy of my salvation,**
> **and uphold me with a willing spirit."**

Opening Prayer (John 12:24)
God of renewal,
> neither troubled soul nor threat of death
>> could stop your Son
>>> from living with passion and purpose,
>>> teaching us to reach for more.

In the teachings of our brother Jesus,
> we behold your glory and learn to face death
> and the unknown unafraid:
>> "Very truly, I tell you,
>> unless a grain of wheat
>> falls into the earth and dies,
>> it remains just a single grain;
>> but if it dies, it bears much fruit."

Help us bear the fruit of new life,
> that you may be glorified
> and all people may come to know your ways.

Amen.

PROCLAMATION AND RESPONSE

Prayer of Confession (Jeremiah 31, Psalm 51:10-11)
Renew us, Lord.
Cleanse us from our sin
> and we will be whiter than snow.

Write your law on our hearts
> and take away our excuses,
>> our feeble protestations
>>> that we know not what we do.

75

Help us stand in your presence,
as women and men
who walk gently upon the earth
and speak lovingly with one another.
We yearn for the time
when guilt will not trouble our sleep,
nor will we feel compelled
to beg excuses for our misdeeds.
Create in us a clean heart, O God,
and put a new and right spirit within us.
Do not cast us away from your presence,
and do not take your Holy Spirit from us.

Assurance of Pardon (Jeremiah 31, Psalm 51)
The One who loves us is faithful,
writing the ways of life on our very hearts.
Look within and know that you are loved
and accepted by our gracious God.

Response to the Word (Jeremiah 31, John 12)
Through Christ, God has written the ways of life
on our hearts.
May we live in the day when we no longer need
to teach one another truths uttered of old.
May we live as those who know the Lord!

Call to Prayer (John 12)
Jesus prayed that God's name would be glorified, and it
was glorified. We pray that God may be glorified, and it
is so. Let us bring our prayers before the Lord, that our
spirits may reflect the love of Christ.

THANKSGIVING AND COMMUNION

Offering Prayer (Jeremiah 31, Psalm 51, John 12)
Nurturing God,
just as you led your people out of Egypt
and gave them the laws of life,

renew your covenant with us
and fill us with the joy of your salvation.
Bless these, our offerings, in the name of the one
who cleanses our hearts and teaches us to live
as those who are not afraid to die. Amen.

SENDING FORTH

Benediction (John 12)
Renewed in God, death has lost its sting.
In God, we bear much fruit.
Restored in Christ, death has lost its sting.
In Christ, we are reflections of God's glory.
Reborn in the Spirit, death has lost its sting.
In the Spirit, we are renewed and made whole.
Go with God's blessing.

CONTEMPORARY OPTIONS

Contemporary Gathering Words (Psalm 51)
We feel tired and worn out.
Renew us, Lord.
Past mistakes weigh heavily upon us.
Wash away our sin.
Petty squabbles distract us.
Make us whiter than snow.
Don't send us away from your presence!
Put your Holy Spirit within us!

Praise Sentences (John 12)
Glorify your name, O God.
All praise to the eternal God.
Glorify your name, O God.
All praise to the living Christ.
Glorify your name, O God.
All praise to the Holy Spirit.

APRIL 1, 2012

Palm / Passion Sunday
Deborah Sokolove

COLOR
Purple

PALM SUNDAY READINGS
Psalm 118:1-2, 19-29; Mark 11:1-11

PASSION SUNDAY READINGS
Isaiah 50:4-9a; Psalm 31:9-16; Philippians 2:5-11;
Mark 14:1–15:47 or Mark 15:1-39, (40-47)

THEME IDEAS
Whether in celebration or in distress, God promises to be
with us. Jesus poured out his life for the healing of the
world, accepting disgrace and shame in faith that the
Holy One would restore him to wholeness. God is revealed in Jesus and in the faith of those who love the
world in the name of Christ. As Jesus trusted in God even
in his most terrible hour, so may we trust in God's steadfast love. The story of Christ's agony and death on the
cross is essential to our understanding of his resurrection.

INVITATION AND GATHERING
Call to Worship (Psalm 118, Mark 11)
Give thanks to the Holy One, for God is good.
God's steadfast love endures forever.

With hosannas and praise,
we greet the One who calls us.
Blessed is the one who comes
in the name of the Most High!
This is the day that God has made.
Let us be glad and rejoice in it!

Opening Prayer (Isaiah 50, Philippians 2, Mark 15)

Steadfast Lover of all creation,
you sent your Holy Child, Jesus,
to teach us how to love one another.
Willingly giving up any claim to power or place,
Jesus poured out his life for the sake of the world,
showing us how to love one another
by the power of his love.
As we stand with those who sang hosanna
at his coming into Jerusalem;
as we gaze with those who looked from a distance
at his death on the cross,
open our ears to the sound of your voice
whispering, "Trust in me, always." Amen.

PROCLAMATION AND RESPONSE

Prayer of Confession (Psalm 31, Mark 15)

Be gracious to us, Holy One, for we are in distress.
Like those who ran away
as Christ was crucified,
we have forgotten your promises,
and our days are ruled by fear.
Like the disciples who in their despair
thought that the death of Jesus
was the end of everything good,
we feel like broken, empty vessels,
afraid to share what we have
lest we be left with nothing.
Our strength fails
when we see the misery around us,

**and we forget our task to love the world
as you have loved us.**
Forgive our weakness and our fears, O God.
**And deliver us from doubt,
that we may put our trust in you
rather than in ourselves.**

Words of Assurance (Psalm 31)
The radiance of God pours over us
even before we ask, melting us like the sun
that warms the earth after a cold, hard winter.
Trusting in God's promise of overflowing grace,
in the name of Christ, you are forgiven.
**In the name of Christ, you are forgiven.
Glory to God. Amen.**

Passing the Peace of Christ
Even as we remember Christ's earthly passion,
we know that Christ is always risen.
May the peace of Christ be with you always.
May the peace of Christ be with you always.

Response to the Word (Mark 15)
Radiant Spirit of Love,
as Mary Magdalene and Mary the mother of James
watched the crucifixion
for signs of Jesus' death,
so may we watch and wait
for signs of his resurrection.
Help us remember that you are always with us,
even when we cannot see you. Amen.

THANKSGIVING AND COMMUNION

Offering Prayer (Isaiah 50, Psalm 31)
God of steadfast love,
even when all seems lost,
you fill us with renewed hope.

Bless these gifts of bread and wine,
> fruit of the vine and work of human hands,
> that they may nourish our hungry souls
>> for the days that are before us,
>> in the name of Christ, who lived and died
>>> and rose again. Amen.

Great Thanksgiving

Christ be with you.
> **And also with you.**

Lift up your hearts.
> **We lift them up to God.**

Let us give our thanks to the Holy One.
> **It is right to give our thanks and praise.**

It is a right, good, and a joyful thing,
> always and everywhere, to give you our thanks,
> Creator of all that is and all that ever shall be.

In the days of the prophets,
> you called your people to trust in you,
> no matter how hopeless the situation,
> no matter how deep their fear or sorrow.

And in your steadfast love,
> you delivered them from their enemies,
> saved them from their oppressors,
> and brought them into a new life
> of justice and peace.

And so, with your people on earth
and all the great cloud of witnesses in heaven,
we praise your name
and join their unending hymn, saying:
> **Holy, holy, holy One, God of power and might,**
>> **heaven and earth are full of your glory.**
> **Hosanna in the highest. Blessed is the one**
>> **who comes your holy name.**
> **Hosanna in the highest.**

Holy are you, and holy is your child, Jesus Christ.

When he entered into Jerusalem to loud hosannas,
  he already knew that he faced betrayal
  at the hand of one he called his friend.
In his last moments, alone and in pain
  and deserted by his followers,
  he still trusted your promise.
(Words of Institution and Memorial Acclamation)

Pour out your Holy Spirit on us gathered here,
  and on these gifts of bread and wine.
Make them be for us the body and blood of Christ,
  that we may become one with Christ,
  one with each other,
  and one in ministry to all the world,
  broken and poured out
  for the healing of the world,
  until all are raised from injustice, misery, and pain.
Steadfast Lover, Trusting Servant, Spirit of Resurrection,
  we praise your holy, eternal, nameless Name.
  Amen.

SENDING FORTH

Benediction (Psalm 118, Mark 11, Mark 15)
Go forth in trust that God is with you.
Bring the hope of new life to a world of despair
in the name of Jesus, who is the Christ.
  Amen.

CONTEMPORARY OPTIONS

Contemporary Gathering Words (Psalm 118, Mark 11)
Greet the Holy One with hosannas and praise.
  Hosanna! All praises to our holy God!

—OR—

Contemporary Gathering Words (Psalm 118, Mark 11)

Open our ears to the sound of your voice
and our eyes to the sight of your glory.

Praise Sentences (Psalm 118, Mark 11)

Blessed is the one who comes
in the name of the Most High!
**Blessed is the one who comes
in the name of the Most High!**

APRIL 5, 2012

Holy Thursday
Mary J. Scifres

COLOR
Purple

SCRIPTURE READINGS
Exodus 12:1-4, (5-10), 11-14; Psalm 116:1-4, 12-19;
1 Corinthians 11:23-26; John 13:1-17, 31b-35

THEME IDEAS
Remembrance weaves all of these scriptures together. The
Exodus passage remembers the Passover of the Hebrew
people as they escaped from bondage in Egypt; the
psalmist remembers God hearing and responding in times
of trouble; Paul remembers Jesus' Last Supper; and John's
Gospel remembers Jesus washing the disciples' feet as
they prepared to celebrate that last Passover feast together. These remembrances are woven together in preparation for the solemn and sorrowful time ahead. Weave
the memories into your worship service this night. We
have woven them into a feast of love, an open-table and
ecumenical alternative to Holy Communion, and a more
informal ritual, allowing for stories, testimonies, songs,
and even footwashing.

INVITATION AND GATHERING

Call to Worship (1 Corinthians 11, John 13)
Come to the table. Come, little children, come.
We gather to listen, to remember, to love,
and even to feast together.
Christ invites us to worship, to sing, and to praise.
We all are welcome at Christ's table of love.

Opening Prayer (1 Corinthians 11, John 13)
Christ of glory and grace,
  we worship this night with gratitude and joy.
For the love that you share,
  we give you thanks.
For the lessons that you teach,
  we offer you our lives in your ongoing story.
For the glory that shines through you,
  we open our hearts to give you praise,
    that you may shine through us.
Guide us as we worship you this night:
  into your glory,
    into your story,
  and into your living memory—
    of all that is wonderful and good,
    all that is difficult and true,
    all that is horrible and sad.
As we share the meal you shared with your disciples,
  may we remember the grief that followed.
Even as we mourn,
  we remember your promise
    to feast with us again in heavenly glory.
(May be followed by a hymn or a familiar song.)

PROCLAMATION AND RESPONSE

Prayer of Confession (Exodus 12, Psalm 116,
1 Corinthians 11, John 13)
When fear holds us in bondage,
  and worry prevents us from following you,
  release us.

When selfishness tempts us to oppress others
and keeps us from serving those in need,
forgive us.
When forgetfulness and thoughtlessness distract us
and keep us from paying heed to your teachings,
awaken us.

Words of Assurance (Psalm 116, John 13)
Little children, Christ calls us to love, serve,
and remember.
As we remember the times that we have failed,
God hears our cries and offers us the cup
of salvation.
Love, serve, remember…
We are God's children, redeemed by Christ's grace.

Passing the Peace of Christ (John 13)
As beloved children of God, we should love one another.
Love one another well as you share signs of forgiveness
and peace.

Response to the Word (1 Corinthians 11, John 13)
*(Testimonies or memories of Christ's presence in our lives may
be shared on this evening in place of a traditional sermon or
homily. Following each testimony or memory shared, all may
respond.)*
As often as we eat and drink together,
we proclaim Christ's death and resurrection
in our midst.
As often as we remember and share together,
we proclaim the mystery of Christ's presence
in our lives.
As often as we serve and love one another,
we live as beloved disciples of Christ.

Prayer of Preparation for Ritual of Footwashing (John 13)
Lord Jesus,
we sit at your feet and remember your humility
when you washed the feet of your disciples.

Humble us,
that we may serve generously
as you have served us.
Wash over us with your grace,
that we may be freed to follow and to love
as you lead us to do.
In hope and trust, we pray. Amen.

THANKSGIVING AND COMMUNION

Invitation to Love Feast (Exodus 12, Psalm 116, 1 Corinthians 11, John 13)
In a rush of confusion and fear,
the Hebrews ate before escaping from Egypt.
In a night of confusion and fear,
Christ's disciples ate before understanding
what he sought to tell them.
In our lives of confusion and fear,
Christ invites us to the table of love and peace.
Come into the light of God's love,
escaping the bondage of confusion and fear.
Come into the light of Christ's wisdom,
freed to serve and to love.
Come to the table. Come to the feast.
All are welcome here.

Prayer of Blessing and Thanksgiving
Gracious God,
pour out your blessings
upon these gifts of food and drink,
that they may become for us a loving celebration
of the community of faith.
Pour out your Holy Spirit upon all of us gathered here,
that we may become vessels of love
and celebrations of your presence in the world.
(Crackers and water, sweet rolls and juice, or even a full meal may be shared around a table or passed from one person to another in the tradition of a Moravian love feast. The offering

may be gathered during the celebration or immediately following.)

Invitation to the Offering (John 13)

As we call upon God, God answers. As we serve in Christ's name, Christ lives. As we give of ourselves, God's love through Christ Jesus is multiplied a hundredfold. Let us share with others the bounty of God's love.

Offering Prayer (Psalm 116, John 13)

Loving God,
> we love you and praise you—
>> for loving us,
>> for trusting us to be your servants,
>> for strengthening us to be your disciples.
> Live and love through these gifts,
>> that others may feast at your table
>> and know of your grace.
> In Christ's name, we pray. Amen.

SENDING FORTH

Benediction (John 13)

Beloved children of God, we have been loved and lifted up by Christ.
We go forth to love and to lift others out of their despair.
May Christ guide us forth to serve.
May loving service be our presence in the world.

CONTEMPORARY OPTIONS

Contemporary Gathering Words (1 Corinthians 11, John 13)

Why have we gathered?
To love, serve, and remember.
Why do we worship?
To love, serve, and remember.

Why do we come to the table?
To love, serve, and remember.
What will we do when we leave this place?
Love, serve, and remember.

Praise Sentences (Psalm 116, John 13)

We gather to serve and to love.
Praise be to God!
We gather to serve and to love.
Praise be to God!

APRIL 6, 2012

Good Friday
Jamie D. Greening

COLOR
Black or None

SCRIPTURE READINGS
Isaiah 52:13–53:12; Psalm 22; Hebrews 10:16-25 (16-23); John 18:1–19:42

THEME IDEAS
Good Friday is the most somber day of the Christian year. It has only one theme and only one event in mind: Jesus' death. The flow of the service should systematically emphasize the progression toward death at Golgotha with the service finally ending on the proclamation that the world got what it wanted. Resist the temptation to point toward the hope that comes at Easter. That is for another day. Today is about the Christian doctrine that Jesus did indeed die, and that his death was painful.

INVITATION AND GATHERING

Call to Worship (Psalm 22)
(With each repetitive phrase, the worship leader should get progressively louder, until the last question is almost a demand.)
Sisters and brothers, why are we here tonight (today)?
To tell what Jesus did in the midst of our brokenness.

Sisters and brothers, why are we here tonight?
To give our praise in the midst of our pain.
Sisters and brothers, why are we here tonight?
To seek the Lord and give God our praise.
Sisters and brothers, why are we here tonight?
**To join with the families of the earth
as we worship the Holy One.**

Opening Prayer (Hebrews 10)
Almighty God,
  we would be lying to you and deceiving ourselves
    if we pretended to be joyful
      and satisfied tonight (today).
We are not.
The violent pain that our friend Christ Jesus endured
  makes us want to hide and wait until it is over;
  it makes us wish to ignore his wounds altogether.
Yet in the miracle of grace, you have drawn us here,
  along with millions of others around the earth,
    that we might remember Christ's once-for-all sacrifice
      and covenant of grace.
As we worship you tonight
  and undertake the ancient work of remembering,
  we ask that you open our hearts to feel anew
    exactly why this is called "Good Friday."
In the name of Christ our Lord, amen.

PROCLAMATION AND RESPONSE

Prayer of Confession (Isaiah 52–53, John 18–19)
(This is designed for two readers. Reader 1 on the chancel and Reader 2 on the sanctuary floor, preferably in the midst of the people.)
He has borne and carried the evil of our hearts.
He has borne my evil.
Because of our transgressions, he was wounded.
**Because of my hate, prejudice, immorality,
greed, lying, intolerance, and blasphemy,
he was wounded.**

92

Our iniquities crushed him and...
(cutting off Reader 1)
>**I crushed him! I drove the nails.**
>**I wove the thorny crown. I pierced his side.**
>**I shouted "crucify him."**
The Lord laid it all on him—
all our iniquity, punishment, and guilt.
He heaped the ugliest part of us
onto his amazing beauty.
>**With every puncture, each whip stroke,**
>**at every cry of anguish**
>**and innumerable flinch of pain,**
>**in every wound and bruise,**
>**he was healing the brokenness**
>**of my sinful soul.**

Words of Assurance (Hebrews 10)
We are guilty, but God is faithful.
In this faithfulness, God chose to remember
our lawlessness no longer.
Through Christ, our sins—yours and mine—
are not only forgiven, they are forgotten.
Christ blotted out the ledger book with his love.

Response to the Word (Isaiah 52-53, John 18-19)
The Word hung between heaven and earth
on a splintery cross. At the place where two wooden
beams intersected, sin and salvation also intersected.
>**It astonishes us—why would Christ do this?**
The Word bled, shouted, and died.
>**He startled us—what kind of love is this?**
The Word has broken our hearts.
>**The tragic sorrow marks our faces with shame.**

THANKSGIVING AND COMMUNION

Invitation to the Offering (Hebrews 10, John 18–19)
Was there anything Jesus did not give, as he died on
Calvary? Did he withhold anything as he set our spirits

free from fear? The answer is no, he gave it all. Now, what will you give, in light of one who died on a tree?

Offering Prayer (Hebrews 10)

As your love brought us healing,
    may our gifts be used to heal.
As your sacrifice brought us salvation,
    may our sacrifices be used to save.
As your offering feeds our souls,
    may our offering feed the hungry.
As you willingly gave yourself,
    may we give faithfully of ourselves.

SENDING FORTH

Benediction (John 18–19)

"Crucify him," they scream,
    and crucify him they do.
Pierce his side and watch him bleed.
Make certain he is dead.
They murder an innocent man on the cross.
We murder him with our sins.
We walk away from here with stained hands
    and bruised hearts.
But it does not matter who did it.
It is Friday. He is dead.
Jesus is dead.
God is dead.
Did we get what we really wanted?
(W. H. Auden's Poem, "Stop All the Clocks" may also be read at the end of this service.)

CONTEMPORARY OPTIONS

Contemporary Gathering Words (Isaiah 53)

Come, behold the man of suffering.
    We have come.
Come, look at his appearance.
    We have come.

Come, gather around the cross to see him.
We have come.
Come, weep as the curtain falls
over the light of the world.
We have come.
We see.
We behold.
We weep.

Praise Sentences (Psalm 22, Isaiah 52–53, John 18–19)
The ironic plaque said it all:
The King of the Jews.
The King of the Jews:
The Lord of the Church.
The King of Kings:
The Lord of Creation,
exalted and lifted up.

APRIL 8, 2012

Easter Sunday
Bill Hoppe

COLOR
White

SCRIPTURE READINGS
Acts 10:34-43; Psalm 118:1-2, 14-24; 1 Corinthians 15:1-11; John 20:1-18 or Mark 16:1-8

THEME IDEAS
Good news—wonderful, amazing news—the best news ever: Jesus Christ is risen from the dead! All of today's readings shout the victory of life and love over death: Peter and Paul share their experience with, and the calling of, the risen Christ; the psalmist foretells the resurrection, the Lord's marvelous doing; and we're present with Mary Magdalene and Peter as they begin to realize the truth that Jesus lives on that first Easter morning. All of history, from the beginning of creation to that moment in the garden tomb, has anticipated this pivotal event, this fulcrum of existence. From this time forward, life will never be the same—life is now as it was meant to be.

INVITATION AND GATHERING
Call to Worship (Psalm 118, Mark 16)
Give thanks to the Lord!
God's love endures forever!

Sing songs of victory! Shout the good news!
Jesus is risen! Christ is risen!
Open the gates of righteousness!
Enter in and give thanks to the Lord!
This is the day the Lord has made!
Hallelujah! Rejoice! Christ is risen!

Opening Prayer (Psalm 118)
We can hardly believe our eyes and ears—the Lord is risen! Let us pray.

Mighty God,
    you have become our strength
      and our salvation.
With Christ,
    you have raised us from the dead.
With Christ,
    you have freed us from the chains of death.
The stone that the builders rejected
    has become the chief cornerstone of our lives.
We marvel at your amazing love, Lord.
We are delirious with joy!
Hear the praises of your people on this day of days!
Amen.

PROCLAMATION AND RESPONSE

Prayer of Confession (John 20, Mark 16)
Lord, we have heard the news,
    yet we haven't listened;
  we have seen the truth,
    yet we haven't understood.
We see the empty tomb,
    but we cannot grasp its truth—
      that death has seen its day.
Though you stand before us and call us by name,
    we can't seem to recognize you.

Roll away the stone of disbelief from our hearts.
Lord of all,
> revive us, resurrect us.

Lord of life,
> we pray in the name of the risen Christ. Amen.

Words of Assurance (Acts 10)

Everywhere and in every circumstance,
> all who seek God and all who seek righteousness
> are embraced by the Lord.

Hear the message of grace and peace,
> of love and forgiveness.

Feel the anointing of the Holy Spirit
> and the power of the resurrection.

Proclaim the wonderful salvation of God.
Celebrate this incredible gift of life! Amen.

Passing the Peace of Christ (1 Corinthians 15)

By the grace of God, we are what we are. By the grace of
God, we live through our risen savior. Share the peace of
Christ with one another as you greet your neighbor in the
Lord.

Response to the Word (Acts 10)

Holy One,
> as your word foretold,
> as all the prophets testified,
> and as all the disciples bore witness,
>> we also affirm what we have seen and heard.

Lord of all,
> grant that we may bring your words of life to all,
> that we may share your love and forgiveness
>> in the name of Christ Jesus. Amen.

THANKSGIVING AND COMMUNION

Offering Prayer (John 20, Mark 16)

Gracious God,
> for saving us from death;
> for opening our tombs

and casting aside our burial garments;
   for all that you have given to us,
     we give you our unending thanks and praise.
In your holy name we pray, amen.

SENDING FORTH

Benediction (Acts 10)

You know the message that God sent to all people,
preaching peace by Jesus Christ—he is Lord of all! That
message spread throughout the world: how Jesus went
about doing good and healing all who were oppressed,
for God was with him. We are witnesses to all that he did
and to his victory over death. Take this good news with
you. Share your great joy with everyone. Christ is risen!
Amen!

CONTEMPORARY OPTIONS

Contemporary Gathering Words (Psalm 118)

It is so good to give thanks to the Lord!
   God's love lasts forever!
Praise God! The Lord has answered our prayer!
   God's love lasts forever!

—OR—

Contemporary Gathering Words (John 20, Mark 16)

At the dawning of the day, we make our way to a cold
tomb. Our eyes are filled with tears of deep sorrow; we
dread what we will find there. To our utter shock and surprise, the stone has been rolled away from the entrance.
The tomb is empty! Something supernatural has hap-
pened. Do we dare believe our eyes? Has the impossible
really taken place? Can we really believe that Jesus lives?
Yes…yes, we can. We must! Glory to God, our savior
lives!

Praise Sentences (Psalm 118)
The Lord is my refuge. God is my deliverer!
God's hands raise me up!
Tell all of God's amazing works!
God's works are wonderful!

APRIL 15, 2012

Second Sunday of Easter
Ken Burton

COLOR
White

SCRIPTURE READINGS
Acts 4:32-35; Psalm 133; 1 John 1:1–2:2; John 20:19-31

THEME IDEAS
In Acts, Luke tells us that the unity of the Church is made manifest by the willingness of its members to share according to the needs of its members. From the First Epistle of John, we learn that those who "miss the mark" may confess and return in God's love; and the author of the Fourth Gospel assures us that all who believe are offered new life in Christ's name.

INVITATION AND GATHERING

Call to Worship (Acts 4, 1 John 1)
Come and share the ample treasure
of new life in Christ.
    We celebrate our unity as God's people.
Christ has died and Christ is risen!
Christ is with us forevermore.
    Christ is our advocate, our helper,
    our comforter in times of need!

Opening Prayer (1 John 1, John 20)
  Luminous Dancing Fountain of Easter,
  we give you thanks as we gather in this place
  to celebrate your love for us
  and for our broken world.
  **Come among us with your power
  and bind us together as your people.**
  Enable us to go forth into the world with great grace,
  empowered as those who have seen and believed.
  Amen.

PROCLAMATION AND RESPONSE

Prayer of Confession (John 20)
  Holy One,
    like doubting Thomas,
      it is often hard for us to believe
        where we have not seen;
      it is even hard for us to accept your love
        when we have known it directly
          and felt the wounds carried by others
            on our behalf.
  Forgive us, we pray,
    for our doubt and our unbelief. Amen.

Words of Assurance (1 John 1)
  Creator God sees our darkness and brings us light.
  Christ, our Savior, knows our failings
    and intercedes on our behalf.
  The Spirit blows through us and offers us peace.

Passing the Peace of Christ (1 John 1, John 20)
  Even as Christ offered himself for us,
  so now we offer his peace to friends and strangers.
  May the Peace of Christ be with you, always.
  May the Peace of Christ be with you, always.

Response to the Word (Psalm 133)
  Generous Source of Life,
  we have heard your word of grace and blessing.

We have felt it running through us,
even as precious oil
ran through Aaron's beard.
May we use the blessing of your holy energy
for renewed service in your name. **Amen**

THANKSGIVING AND COMMUNION

Invitation to the Offering (Acts 4)
May we who have received much give generously as we
collect this morning's offering.

Offering Prayer (John 20)
Holy One, how gracious you have been
in your gifts to us!
Bless these, our gifts to you.
May our lives embody your love for us,
that we may be united as your people.
Amen.

SENDING FORTH

Benediction (Psalm 133)
How good and pleasant it is
when kindred live together in unity!
How great and powerful it is
when they go forth to serve.
Let us leave this place,
knowing ourselves to be bearers of God's peace
and instruments of God's love.
Amen.

CONTEMPORARY OPTIONS

Contemporary Gathering Words (Acts 4, 1 John 1)
Come and share the ample treasure of God's love.
Join us as we celebrate new life in Christ.

Praise Sentences (1 John 1, John 20)
Christ is up and death is down!
Jesus lives! Give him the crown!

APRIL 22, 2012

Third Sunday of Easter

B. J. Beu

COLOR
White

SCRIPTURE READINGS
Acts 3:12-19; Psalm 4; 1 John 3:1-7; Luke 24:36b-48

THEME IDEAS
Seeing is believing; but believing is also seeing. In Acts, Peter admonishes the crowd for being amazed at the miraculous healing performed in Christ's name. The power they have witnessed comes from the God of Abraham, Isaac, and Jacob—the same God who raised Jesus from the dead. The psalmist calls out with hope in the midst of distress, for in God hope can always be found. The Epistle speaks of the hope that comes from being in Christ and being known by God, even as Christ is known. Finally, the Gospel beseeches us to see and believe and to have hope in the face of death. For God is greater than death, bringing forgiveness of sins and newness of life to those who believe.

INVITATION AND GATHERING

Call to Worship (Luke 24)
See and you will believe.
Believe and you will see.

In the midst of our sorrow and grief,
Christ comes to ease our pain.
See and you will believe.
Believe and you will see.
  In the midst of our doubt and fear,
Christ comes to bring us hope.
See and you will believe.
Believe and you will see.
  In the midst of our sickness unto death,
Christ comes to bring us life.

Opening Prayer (1 John 3)

Merciful God,
    you come to us in our darkness
      and fill us with your light;
    you come to us in our weakness
      and do not put us to shame;
    you come to us as we wander like orphans
      and call us your children.
Help us purify ourselves, as Christ is pure,
    that we may be fit vessels
      to carry your light to the world. Amen.

PROCLAMATION AND RESPONSE

Prayer of Confession (Luke 24)

Tender, loving God,
    when Jesus appeared to his disciples,
      he showed them the wounds
        on his hands and feet,
        and shared with them
          a meal of broiled fish.
We long to see you as you are,
    that we too may see and believe.
Forgive our lack of faith.
Teach us to first believe
    where we have not seen,

that in believing
    we may truly see.
Come to us in our moments of doubt and loss,
    and give us joy in the knowledge
        of your everlasting love. Amen.

Assurance of Pardon (Luke 24)
Jesus appeared again and again to his disciples
    until they found the faith they needed
    to embrace the fullness of God's power
    and salvation.
Open your eyes to the presence of Christ in our midst.
Feel his power and accept the salvation he brings.
In Christ we are forgiven. Amen.

Response to the Word (Acts 3)
Abraham and Sarah believed God and found life.
Isaac and Rebecca believed God and found life.
Jacob and Rachel believed God and found life.
Believe in the Holy One and you will find life.

THANKSGIVING AND COMMUNION

Offering Prayer (Psalm 4)
O God,
    your love gladdens the heart
        more than the choicest bread
        and the finest wine.
As you have filled us with every good thing,
    we offer you our thankfulness
        in these, our gifts. Amen.

SENDING FORTH

Benediction (Luke 24)
Go as witnesses of the risen Lord.
Christ has fed us and made us whole.
Go as witnesses of the risen Lord.
Christ has brought us joy.

Go as witnesses of the risen Lord.
Christ has given us the kingdom.

—*OR*—

Benediction (Acts 3)
May the God of Abraham and Sarah
bless you and keep you.
We go with God's blessings.
May the God of Isaac and Rebecca
shine upon your life.
We go with God's blessings.
May the God of Jacob and Rachel
be gracious unto you.
We go with God's blessings.
May the God of Jesus Christ
grant you peace.

CONTEMPORARY OPTIONS

Contemporary Gathering Words (1 John 3)
What do you see when you look in the mirror?
We see children of God.
But who will you become?
We will become like Jesus
when we see him as he is.
How will you get there?
We will purify ourselves
as Christ is pure.
Come! Let us worship God.

Praise Sentences (Acts 3, Luke 24)
Praise the One who heals the sick.
Praise the One who raises the dead.
Praise the One who restores sight to the blind.
Christ is risen!
Christ is risen!
Christ is risen indeed!

APRIL 29, 2012

Fourth Sunday of Easter
Mary Petrina Boyd

COLOR

White

SCRIPTURE READINGS

Acts 4:5-12; Psalm 23; 1 John 3:16-24; John 10:11-18

THEME IDEAS

The fourth Sunday of Easter is Good Shepherd Sunday, and each year the scripture readings include the twenty-third Psalm and a reading from John 10, describing Jesus as the Good Shepherd. The image of Jesus assures us that we are known and cared for. In Acts, Peter affirms Jesus' power to heal and names Jesus as the cornerstone of faith. First John points to the human response to the Shepherd's love, reminding us to love one another in truth and action.

INVITATION AND GATHERING

Call to Worship (Psalm 23)

Come, walk in green pastures.
We follow the Shepherd.
Come, lie down in green pastures.
We trust the Shepherd.
Come, dine at the table of abundance.
We are fed by the Shepherd.

Come, dwell in God's house.
We live in the Shepherd's care.

Opening Prayer (Psalm 23, John 10)
Loving Shepherd,
 you know our names;
 you care for us.
When we face darkness and death,
 walk beside us.
When we hunger for your love,
 fill us with your presence.
When we are fearful,
 feed us at your table.
May we dwell in the house of goodness and mercy
 all the days of our lives. Amen.

PROCLAMATION AND RESPONSE

Prayer of Confession (Psalm 23, 1 John)
Good Shepherd,
 we take your care for granted.
In the midst of your many blessings,
 we complain of not having enough.
In the presence of danger,
 we fail to trust your abiding love.
When you set a table before us,
 we turn aside from you.
Call us back into your care
 and help us trust your caring presence,
 that our actions may proclaim your truth. Amen.

Words of Assurance (Psalm 23)
Surely goodness and mercy shall follow us
 all the days of our lives.
God forgives our failures and calls us back
 into the flock.

Passing the Peace of Christ (1 John 3)
God calls us to love one another as God loves us. In this

we know the truth of Christ's peace. Share signs of Christ's peace with one another.

Response to the Word (Psalm 23, John 10, 1 John 3)

Good Shepherd,
>we are the sheep of your pasture,
>you know us by name.

We offer grateful thanks for your loving care.

Open our hearts and minds
>to the guiding of your Spirit in our lives.

Lead us in right paths,
>that we may serve you in truth and action. Amen.

THANKSGIVING AND COMMUNION

Invitation to the Offering (Psalm 23, 1 John 3)

The Shepherd cares for us, providing all that we need in abundance. The Shepherd calls us to love one another in truth and action. May our gifts reflect our trust in the Shepherd's care. May our offerings show our willingness to love one another.

Offering Prayer (Psalm 23, 1 John 3)

God of love,
>you abide with us;
>you provide for all our needs
>>and guide us in your ways.

Out of gratitude for your care,
>we bring our gifts before you.

Use them for your work of caring,
>that all may feast at the table of abundance,
>>walk without fear,
>>>and drink deeply
>>>>from the cup of compassion. Amen.

Invitation to Communion (Psalm 23, John 10)

God prepares the table for us, offering us a feast of abundant love. Our cups overflow with the bounty of grace, for our Shepherd knows us as no one else can—restoring our souls, healing our brokenness, nourishing us with bread and cup for the life of ministry. Come to the table and feast with the Shepherd.

SENDING FORTH

Benediction (1 John 3)
Nourished by the Shepherd's abundant love,
   go forth to walk in the paths of righteousness.
Love one another in truth and action.
May God's abundant blessings abide in you forever.

CONTEMPORARY OPTIONS

Contemporary Gathering Words (Acts 4, Psalm 23)
Come to the shepherd!
   Walk in the paths of righteousness.
Come to Jesus Christ, the cornerstone!
   Ground your life in Jesus.
Come to the Spirit, who abides in us!
   Feast at the table of joy!

Praise Sentences (Acts 4, 1 John 3)
God is our shepherd! God cares for us.
   Jesus Christ is the cornerstone!
   He is the foundation of our lives.
The Spirit abides in us!
   And we abide in the Spirit.

MAY 6, 2012

Fifth Sunday of Easter
Mary J. Scifres

COLOR
White

SCRIPTURE READINGS
Acts 8:26-40; Psalm 22:25-31; 1 John 4:7-21; John 15:1-8

THEME IDEAS
Abiding in Christ's love is the key to sharing Christ's love with others. An angel visits Philip, and Philip goes where he is sent—transforming the life of the Ethiopian eunuch as Philip shares time and testimony with him. See what love is given when we share the good news of Christ! John writes of love, deepening the challenge as he reminds us that Christ's love is perfected in us only when we allow that love to cast out all fear and dare to love every brother and sister we meet. Jesus comforts us with the reminder that, as our vine, he is always connected to us, sustaining and nurturing us as we grow in love, as we reach toward perfect love of God and neighbor, and as we trust that we can indeed rest in the abiding love of God.

INVITATION AND GATHERING

Call to Worship (John 15)
Come to the vineyard of God.
We seek Christ, the vine of great love.

Drink from the waters of life.
We live in the light of God's grace.
Come to the vineyard of God.
All are welcome here.

Opening Prayer (John 15)

God of love,
plant us in the soil of your grace.
Nurture us with the strength of Christ,
the vine of everlasting life.
Enlighten us with the wisdom of your Spirit,
which flows through us today and all days.
Abide in us,
that we may abide in you
and live in your love.
In your holy name, we pray. Amen.

PROCLAMATION AND RESPONSE

Prayer of Confession (1 John 4)

Merciful One,
you know when we are afraid to love;
you know when we are too cowardly
to show mercy.
Remind us again
that perfect love casts out such fears.
Surround us and strengthen us with your perfect love,
even in the face of our imperfections.
Imbue us with a love so strong,
with such growth toward perfection,
that we may cast aside our pride
and embrace the power of love.

Words of Assurance (John 15)

Christ is the vine. We are simply branches.
If we abide in Christ, Christ's words will abide in us.
Ask for whatever you wish in Christ's name
and it will be granted.

In the name of Christ,
   you who seek forgiveness are forgiven!
   In the name of Christ,
   you who seek forgiveness are forgiven!

Passing the Peace of Christ (1 John 4, John 15)

Abiding in Christ's love, let us turn to one another and offer signs of forgiveness, love and peace.

Prayer in Response to the Word or Opening Prayer (1 John 4, John 15)

Abide with us and within us, O Holy One.
Transform us into branches of your love,
   bearing fruit that feeds and nourishes a world
      hungry for kindness and compassion.
Strengthen us that we may grow into your likeness
   with courage and conviction.
Live in us, that we may live in you,
   and live as your abiding presence in the world.
In faith and trust, we pray. Amen.

THANKSGIVING AND COMMUNION

Invitation to the Offering (1 John 4)

Christ reminds us that lovers of God must be lovers of people. And so, we are invited to show our love as we offer ourselves and our gifts to Christ, to Christ's church, and to one another. May we share freely and generously the love and abundance that God has given us.

Offering Prayer (1 John 4, John 15)

Beloved Father, Beloved Mother,
   Beloved Generous God,
   abide not only in us,
      but in the gifts we now return to you.
Let your abundant love flow through these offerings,
   that others may know and experience
      your constant, abiding love.
In Christ's name, we pray. Amen.

The Great Thanksgiving (An Act of Preparation for Holy Communion, 1 John 4, John 15)

The Lord be with you.
And also with you.
Lift up your hearts.
We lift them up to the Lord.
Let us give thanks to the Lord our God.
It is right to give our thanks and praise.
It is right, and a good and joyful thing,
always and everywhere to give thanks to you,
almighty God, creator of heaven and earth.
In ancient days, you created us in your image,
inviting us to live as your people upon this earth.
When we fell short and acted out of fear and doubt,
you held our hand and walked with us
out of the garden and into every corner
of the earth.
When we struggled to love,
you blessed us and challenged us
to be a blessing to all the nations.
You continue to extend the hand
of your steadfast love, abiding with us always,
even when we turn away.
In the words of the prophets, you challenged us
to live in love and righteousness.
But as we shrunk from the challenge,
you sent your Son, Christ Jesus,
as love for a love-starved world.
From the earliest days of creation,
to the most recent of days,
you offer to abide in us
even as we abide in your love.
And so, with your people on earth,
and all the company of heaven,
we praise your name
and join their unending hymn, saying:

Holy, holy, holy Lord, God of power and might,
  heaven and earth are full of your glory.
Hosanna in the highest. Blessed is the one
  who comes in the name of the Lord.
Hosanna in the highest.
Holy are you and blessed is your constant love.

Through Christ's patient love and unfailing grace,
  we are once again invited into your abiding love
  and rescued from the fears and sins
  that would separate us
  from your nurturing presence.
With Christ's love in our lives,
  we are invited to live in your love
  and to reveal your love to the world,
  even as we proclaim the mystery of faith.
  Christ has died.
  Christ is risen.
  Christ will come again.

With joy and gratitude, we break this bread of life
  and remember the many times when Jesus' love
  was shared in the breaking of the bread.
In remembrance, we will take and eat this bread.
With awe and wonder, we fill this cup
  and remember the many times
  when Jesus poured out his love
  as an everlasting spring of grace.
In remembrance, we will drink from this cup
  and partake of the love that overflows in our lives.

Communion Prayer (John 15)
Pour out your Holy Spirit on all of us gathered here,
  that we may be the branches of Christ,
  your true vine.
Pour out your Holy Spirit
  on these gifts of bread and wine
  that we may be filled with your abiding love.

Strengthen us in the power of your Holy Spirit,
   that we may be one with Christ,
   one with each other,
   and one in ministry to all the world,
   until Christ comes in final victory
   and we feast at the heavenly banquet.
Through Jesus Christ, with the Holy Spirit
   in your holy Church, all honor and glory is yours,
   almighty God, now and forevermore. **Amen.**

Giving the Bread and Cup
(The bread and wine are given to the people, with these or other words of blessing.)
The life of Christ, living in you.
The love of Christ, loving through you.

SENDING FORTH

Benediction (1 John 4, John 15)
Beloved children of God, love one another well.
   We will abide in Christ's generous love.
Be born in the Spirit of grace.
   We will live in the fullness of hope.
Grow into branches bearing the fruit of love:
peace, joy, hope, faith.
   **We will remember that the greatest harvest
   is the harvest of love.**

CONTEMPORARY OPTIONS

Contemporary Gathering Words (1 John 4)
Love one another, my friends.
   For God is love in us.
Love even the stranger well.
   For God is love in us.
Love sister and brother and child.
   For God is love in us.
Love one another, my friends.
   For God is love in us.

Contemporary Gathering Words or Response to the Word (Psalm 22, 1 John 4)
As the weak realize their strength;
as the poor eat and are satisfied,
God's love abides in us.
As the stranger finds a friend;
as the family offers forgiveness,
God's love abides in us.
As the ends of the earth know of Christ's grace,
God's love abides in us.
(May lead into the Opening Prayer or Unison Prayer in Response to the Word.)

Praise Sentences (1 John 4)
God is love!
God is love!
God is love in us!
God is love in us!

Praise Sentences (Psalm 22)
Praise our God!
Praise our God!
Praise our God forever!

MAY 13, 2012

*Sixth Sunday of Easter / Festival of the
Christian Home / Mother's Day*

Rebecca Gaudino

COLOR

White

SCRIPTURE READINGS

Acts 10:44-48; Psalm 98; 1 John 5:1-6; John 15:9-17

THEME IDEAS

God's love creates a generous dwelling place. John writes of
Jesus' love as a reality in which we abide, even as we provide this abode for others. This abode of love is a place of joy
as well as of obedience given willingly—not out of the fear
that separates servant from master, but out of the understanding that grows between friends: Jesus and his disciples.
First John describes an even closer relationship: believers are
born to our parent God. The story of Cornelius's baptism
adds the detail of spaciousness: the abode of love welcomes
all peoples. The psalmist expands God's caring attention beyond the house of Israel to the entire globe!

INVITATION AND GATHERING

Call to Worship (Psalm 98)
Sing to God a new song,
for God has done marvelous things!

Make a joyful noise to God, all the earth,
    for God is still doing marvelous things!
Break into joyful song!
    **Sing praises with lyre and melody
    and trumpets!**
Let the seas roar and the floods clap their hands!
    **For God is coming to judge the world
    with righteousness.**
God is coming to judge the world with equity.
    Sing to God a new song!

Opening Prayer (Acts 10, Psalm 98, 1 John 5, John 15)
God of songs and marvels, old and new,
    your powerful love for this world
        continues to astound us.
In these last days of Easter,
    we gather to recall the love
        that brought Jesus into this world
            and into our lives:
                as savior, friend, and brother.
We thank you for welcoming us into your household
    and for trusting us with your marvelous work
        to draw all people into the spacious home
            of your love. Amen.

PROCLAMATION AND RESPONSE

Prayer of Confession (John 15)
Jesus, friend and brother,
    you taught us to abide in your generous love,
        for it completes our lives and gives us joy;
    you ask us to love others as you have loved us,
        for it brings your creation to fruition.
We sometimes struggle
    to love the people in our lives
        as you have loved us.
Forgive us, we pray,
    and teach us your love again. Amen.

Words of Assurance (John 15:15b-16a)

Long ago Jesus said to his disciples,
"I have called you friends, because I have made
known to you everything that I have heard from [God].
You did not choose me, but I chose you!"
Jesus speaks these words to us today.
Jesus forgives us and chooses us to be his friends,
sharing his great work of love. Hallelujah!

Passing the Peace of Christ (John 15)

Meet the friends of Jesus! Turn and greet your brothers
and sisters with the peace, love, and joy of Jesus the
Christ.

Response to the Word (Acts 10, John 15)

God of Love,
do not let us grow weary of living our lives
according to the example of your child, Jesus.
Loving one another is a great challenge
and a high calling.
We do not want to fail our friend and brother.
Pour out upon us your Spirit
who reminds us that we bear Jesus' love and life
within our very being—
a powerful gift for our world.
Out of this gift, may we bear the fruit of love. Amen.

THANKSGIVING AND COMMUNION

Invitation to the Offering (Acts 10, Psalm 98, John 15)

We began our worship today with a psalm about the new
songs that God inspires us to sing. In our Gospel lesson,
we heard Jesus teaching his disciples a new song: a love
song about Jesus' love for his disciples and for the world.
Jesus hoped we would all join in singing and living out
this new song of love. Today in giving to others, let us join
in this song so that the whole world may hear the beautiful and welcoming melody of God's love.

Offering Prayer (Acts 10, John 15)
Pour your Spirit upon these gifts, O God.
Send them into the world
    as a sign and song of your joyous work of love.
Use them to call and welcome into your house of love
    all who are *your* friends
        and *our* brothers and sisters. Amen.

SENDING FORTH

Benediction (John 15:12)
Jesus speaks again today:
    "This is my commandment,
    that you love one another
    as I have loved you."
Go in joy and faithfulness, knowing that you,
the chosen friends of Jesus, abide in Jesus' love
and bear the gift of this love to the world. Amen.

CONTEMPORARY OPTIONS

Contemporary Gathering Words (Psalm 98, John 15)
Are you looking for the joy that completes your life?
Are you hoping for the love that makes a difference
    and gives you a great purpose?
Then welcome to the house of God!
Welcome to the love of God!

—OR—

Contemporary Gathering Words (Psalm 98)
Come, sing a new song to God!
    Remember all the times full of wonder
    God has already saved us!
Plug in the keyboard; tune up those guitars;
try out the drums!
    Make a joyful noise to God, all the earth!
Open the windows! Listen to the choirs outdoors,
feathered and furred!
    Let the hills sing together for joy!

For God is not done doing wonders!
God is coming to set everything right.
Sing a new song to God!

Praise Sentences (Psalm 98)
Praise God with the heavens.
Praise God with the seas.
Praise God with all creation.
Praise God.
Praise God.
Praise God.
(B. J. Beu)

MAY 20, 2012

Ascension Sunday
B. J. Beu

COLOR

White

SCRIPTURE READINGS

Acts 1:1-11; Psalm 47; Ephesians 1:15-23; Luke 24:44-53

THEME IDEAS

Ascension Sunday is about a power that lies beyond our ordinary existence. Through the same power that raised Jesus from the dead and heals us body and soul, we receive the gifts of the Holy Spirit. As Jesus is lifted up to the heavens, we are reminded to look beyond earthly power to the power of the Most High God.

INVITATION AND GATHERING

Call to Worship (Psalm 47:1, 6)

Clap your hands, people of God.
    Shout to God with loud songs of joy.
Sing your praises, people of God.
    Sing praises to our king, sing praises.
Look to the heavens, people of God.
    See the power of the Most High God.
Clap your hands, people of God.
    Shout to God with loud songs of joy.

Opening Prayer (Acts 1, Luke 24)

Most High God,
    as Christ ascended into the heavens,
      may our hearts ascend to you.
Open our eyes to the power of your Spirit,
    that we may strive for more
      than the pedestrian ways of this world.
Open our lives to the fullness of your power,
    that we may be clothed with power from on high.
Help us wait patiently for the baptism of your Spirit,
    that we may be found worthy of your great gifts.
Amen.

PROCLAMATION AND RESPONSE

Prayer of Confession (Acts 1, Ephesians 1, Luke 24)

Merciful God,
    when offered the promise
      of your glorious inheritance,
      we settle for so much less.
Rather than lifting our gaze to see and live
    with the eyes of our hearts enlightened,
      our eyes are fixed on the ground;
      our hearts are set on earthly power;
      our aspirations are limited to getting ahead.
Forgive us.
Teach us anew to wait for your Holy Spirit,
    that we may be clothed with power from on high,
    in the name of the one who ascended to heaven
      to show us the way to live here on earth. Amen.

Assurance of Pardon (Acts 1, Ephesians 1, Luke 24)

When we have the patience and the courage
    to wait, empty, for your Spirit, O God,
      you justify the hope to which we have been called,
      you fill us with your Spirit,
      forgive our transgressions,
      and clothe us with power from on high.

Response to the Word (Ephesians 1:17-19)
Hear anew these words of Paul: "I pray that the God of our Lord Jesus Christ, the [God] of glory, may give you a spirit of wisdom and revelation as you come to know [the Lord], so that, with the eyes of your heart enlightened, you may know what is the hope to which [God] has called you, what are the riches of [God's] glorious inheritance among the saints, and what is the immeasurable greatness of [God's] power for us who believe, according to the working of [God's] great power."

THANKSGIVING AND COMMUNION

Offering Prayer (Psalm 47)
O God,
we praise you for your power and might;
we praise you for your love and mercy;
we praise you for giving us your Spirit;
we praise you for your every blessing.
In gratitude and thanksgiving ,
for all we have received from your hand,
we return to you the fruit of our industry,
in the name of the one who ascended to heaven,
that we might have fullness of life
here on earth. Amen.

SENDING FORTH

Benediction (Luke 24)
Lift up your eyes to the heavens.
Christ ascended to show us the way.
Trust in the power of the Spirit.
Christ ascended to clothe us with power.
Go as witnesses of the risen Lord.
Christ ascended to bring us eternal life.

CONTEMPORARY OPTIONS

Contemporary Gathering Words (Acts 1, Luke 24)

Are you ready to receive the Spirit?
When will it come?
God alone appoints the time.
We are ready.
Are you ready to be clothed with power from on high?
We are ready.
Look to Christ, who calls us to wait and be ready.
We are ready.

Praise Sentences (Psalm 47:6-7)

Sing praises to God, sing praises.
Sing praises to our king, sing praises.
Our God is king over all the earth.
Sing praises with shouts of joy, sing praises.
Sing praises to God, sing praises.
Sing praises to our king, sing praises.

MAY 27, 2012

Pentecost Sunday
Mary J. Scifres

COLOR
Red

SCRIPTURE READINGS
Acts 2:1-21; Psalm 104:24-34, 35b; Romans 8:22-27;
John 15:26-27, 16:4b-15

THEME IDEAS
Although Pentecost is often viewed as the "birthday celebration" of the Church, we do not always recognize how
vivid the images of new birth are in the stories related to
Pentecost. Indeed, the true promise of Pentecost is that we
are all given birth and new life through the Spirit. In Acts,
the followers of Christ are gathered together in one place
when the Holy Spirit comes like a mighty wind and creates a new community of faith and hope, giving birth to
Christ's Church. In Psalm 104, the Spirit speaks and the
creatures of the earth are created, born of God's very
Spirit. In Romans, all of creation groans in labor pains for
new birth and life in the Spirit. Even in John, Jesus prepares the disciples to receive the Advocate, who will
speak truth and new life that they do not yet comprehend.
The pinnacle of Jesus' resurrection story is the new life
given to Jesus' followers—not just in the hereafter, but in

the here and now. This re-birth, this new life, is the promise and the gift of Pentecost.

INVITATION AND GATHERING

Call to Worship (Acts 2, Psalm 104, Romans 8)
Call upon God's holy name.
For in calling, we are saved.
Listen for the wind of the Spirit.
**For in listening, we will hear the Spirit
who brings new life.**
Hope in the promises of Christ.
**We wait, we hope, we worship—
for just as Christ came in days long gone,
so Christ comes to us even now
in the power of the Spirit!**

Opening Prayer (Acts 2)
Come, Holy Spirit, come.
Blow through our lives
with the breath of life.
Blow through our church
with the power of prophecy.
Blow through our world
with the promise of peace and justice.
Work in us even now,
that we may be your people on earth,
your Church,
your work of the Spirit.
Gather all peoples together,
that all may know of your powerful
and life-giving love. Amen.

PROCLAMATION AND RESPONSE

Call to Confession (Romans 8)
Even as we approach God to admit our shortcomings and
sins, the Spirit intercedes for us with sighs of love and
courageous wisdom too deep for words, too amazing for

comprehension. Let us pray silently the confessions of our souls or simply be still, for God knows our very hearts and listens to the Spirit's holy wisdom.
(A time of silence may follow.)

Prayer of Confession (Acts 2, Romans 8)

Spirit of gentleness,
    whisper words of assurance and mercy to us.
As we reflect upon the many ways
    that we do not live out the new life you offer,
        forgive us.
Refresh us to be your people.
Renew us to be your Church.
Rebirth the hope and faith that help us live
    as children of vision and parents of wisdom.
Strengthen our courage
    to be brothers and sisters of Christ
        in unity and love with all of creation.

Words of Assurance (Acts 2)

All who call upon God's holy name are saved.
As we call, God hears; God loves; God forgives.
In the name of Christ, we are all forgiven.
Thanks be to God!

Passing the Peace of Christ (Acts 2)

Gathered together as one, let us share in the joy of that first Pentecost Sunday. Speak words of love. Share signs of peace. For the language of love and peace is universal!

Scripture Drama (Acts 2:14-21)

Leader 1:   When the day of Pentecost had come, they were all together in one place.

Leader 2:   And suddenly from heaven there came a sound like the rush of a violent wind, and it filled the entire house where they were sitting.

(Wait for sound or music effects.)

        Divided tongues, as of fire, appeared among them, and a tongue rested on each of them.

All of them were filled with the Holy Spirit and began to speak in other languages, as the Spirit gave them ability.

Actors: *(speaking in native languages)* **God is good! All the time!**

Leader 1: Now there were devout Jews from every nation under heaven living in Jerusalem.

(Wait for sound or music effects to repeat.)

And at this sound the crowd gathered and was bewildered, because each one heard them speaking in the native language of each.

Actors: *(speaking in native languages)* **And all the time! God is good!**

Thomas: Are not all these who are speaking Galileans? And how is it that I hear in my own native tongue when I am not from Galilee?

Matthew: This is amazing and astounding! We're all hearing in languages we can understand!

Leader 2: The Parthians and the Mexicans spoke and were understood. The Medes and the politicians listened and learned. The Elamites and the children proclaimed and were respected for their wisdom. The residents of care centers and the outspoken teenagers spoke and were truly heard.

Leader 1: From Mesopotamia and the Middle East, from Judea and South Africa, from Cappadocia and Haiti, from Pontus and Bosnia, from Asia and Australia, from Phrygia and Indonesia, from Pamphylia and Tonga, from Egypt and Libya, from Rome and from Calcutta, Jews and Muslims are proclaiming God's great deeds, Christians and Hindus are praising God's great love and Spirit— and they all hear in their own languages.

Actors:	*(speaking native languages)* **God has done great things for me!**
Leader 2:	All were amazed and perplexed that they could speak and hear about God's amazing deeds of power, so clearly and with mysterious comprehension.
Mary:	What does this mean?!
Maria:	*(in Spanish)* What does this mean?!
Lydia:	What does this mean?!
Paul:	*(in Korean)* What does this mean?!
Thomas:	What does this mean?!
Alena:	*(in Tongan)* What does this mean?!
Cyrus:	*(cynically)* What does this mean? These men are drunk, pure and simple. They've clearly been enjoying the fermented fruit of the vine!
Peter:	*(standing with those who have spoken)* "[People] of Judea and all who live in Jerusalem, let this be known to you, and listen to what I say. Indeed, these are not drunk, as you suppose, for it is only nine o'clock in the morning. No, this is what was spoken through the prophet Joel":
Joel:	"In the last days it will be, God declares, that I will pour out my Spirit upon all flesh. Your sons and your daughters shall prophesy; your young men shall see visions, and your old men shall dream dreams. Even upon my servants, both men and women, in those days I will pour out my Spirit; and they shall prophesy. And I will show portents in the heaven above and signs on the earth below, blood, and fire, and smoky mist. The sun shall be turned to darkness and the moon to blood, before the coming of the Lord's great and glorious day. Then everyone who calls on the name of the Lord shall be saved."

Actors: *(speaking in native languages)* **God is Good! All the time. And all the time! God is good!**

Response to the Word (John 15)

The Spirit of truth has come.
May our hearts and minds
    know and understand the truth
    God is revealing to us
        each and every day.

THANKSGIVING AND COMMUNION

Invitation to the Offering (Acts 2, Romans 8)

Freely and abundantly, the Spirit has poured gifts into our lives. We are invited to return those gifts, that others may know the new life available through the power of God's Holy Spirit and the grace of Jesus Christ.

Offering Prayer (Psalm 104, John 15)

O God,
    how amazing are the works of your creation,
    the gift of your presence in our lives
        and in our world!
We praise you and thank you,
    even as we return a portion of these gifts to you.
Send forth your Spirit in and through these gifts,
    that your loving presence may be felt and known
        through every ministry, every life,
            and every need touched by these gifts.
In Christ's name, we pray. Amen

SENDING FORTH

Benediction (Acts 2, Romans 8)

Go forth in the power of the Holy Spirit!
**We go with the strength of God's holy wind
blowing through our lives.**
Speak the truth of love and the miracle of forgiveness.
May we see visions and dream dreams.

May your lives reflect the very presence of God.
**We go as children of the Spirit,
to share Christ's mercy and grace.**

CONTEMPORARY OPTIONS

Contemporary Gathering Words (Acts 2, Romans 8)
Come, Holy Spirit, come.
Speak to our empty lives.
Come, Holy Spirit, come.
Breathe life into our dying dreams.
Come, Holy Spirit, come.
Refresh our fading hopes.
Come, Holy Spirit, come.
Inspire our church with vision.
Come, Holy Spirit, come.
Pour out your power and love.
Come, Holy Spirit, come.
As we worship, inflame us
with wisdom and purpose.

Praise Sentences (Psalm 104)
Rejoice in the creation of life!
Praise God's wonderful works!
Rejoice in the creation of life!
Praise God's wonderful works!

JUNE 3, 2012

Trinity Sunday
Joanne Carlson Brown

COLOR
White

SCRIPTURE READINGS
Isaiah 6:1-8; Psalm 29; Romans 8:12-17; John 3:1-17

THEME IDEAS
1+1+1=1 is a hard concept to grasp. Just ask anyone who has tried to explain the Trinity. The readings for today speak of the various aspects of the Godhead: God in all God's glory and majesty, Christ as guide and teacher, and the Spirit who enlivens us all. We are born in the Spirit, are adopted as sons and daughters of God, and are co-heirs with Christ. The Trinity touches all aspects of our lives as today's readings attest. Holy, Holy, Holy, indeed.

INVITATION AND GATHERING

Call to Worship (Isaiah 6, Romans 8, John 3)
We come this morning to praise God, the three in one.
  Holy, Holy, Holy is the God of hosts.
  Heaven and earth are full of God's glory.
We come embracing our adoption
as sons and daughters of God.
  We rejoice in our identity
  and our new birth in the Spirit.

Let us come before our God
with praise and thanksgiving.
Let us worship the God of glory and love.

Opening Prayer (Isaiah 6, Romans 8)
God of love,
we come this morning with hearts full of praise;
we come with deepest gratitude to you
for adopting us as your sons and daughters.
Help us feel the Spirit move within our lives,
not only during our worship,
but in every aspect of our days.
Help us respond to your loving Spirit
with a full-throated, "Here am I, send me."
May our time together bless us, inspire us,
and lead us in your pathways. Amen.

PROCLAMATION AND RESPONSE

Prayer of Confession (Isaiah 6, Romans 8, John 3)
God of call and new birth,
sometimes we are so filled
with awe at your presence
that we think we are unworthy of you.
Help us remember that you are the God of love—
the one who has birthed us again and again
into new life as adopted sons and daughters.
Forgive us when we doubt our identity.
Forgive us when we shrink from your call
or feel inadequate as your children.
Forgive us for not understanding your full identity
as the one who creates us, calls us, loves us,
saves us, inspires us, sustains us.
Help us say Holy, Holy, Holy, Abba,
and know that you are three in one. Amen.

Words of Assurance (John 3)
God so loved the world, and not just the world,
but each and every one of us,

that God sent Jesus into the world
to bring the message of love, forgiveness,
and salvation.
Know that you are loved and treasured
beyond measure as a true child of God.

Prayer of Preparation (Isaiah 6, John 3)
May our hearts be open to these words of grace.
May we see with new eyes
and hear with enlivened ears
the call to live our lives in accordance
with the Spirit who gives us new birth.

Response to the Word (Isaiah 6, John 3)
Holy, Holy, Holy is the God of hosts whose word comes to
us, touches our lips and hearts, and inspires us to hear and
answer the call to new birth.

THANKSGIVING AND COMMUNION

Invitation to the Offering (Romans 8)
We have received the spirit of new birth and adoption. Let
us respond with gratitude for this gift and for the gift of
salvation, through the one who creates and liberates us,
the one who completes and perfects us, and the one who
comforts and sustains us.

Offering Prayer (Romans 8, John 3)
O God of new birth,
we offer ourselves and our gifts
in deepest gratitude for all your gifts.
May we use them to spread the word of your love,
your grace, and your call to all the world.
Through our gifts,
may others claim their true identity
as your children;
and may they live into that identity
with integrity and thankfulness. Amen.

SENDING FORTH

Benediction (Isaiah 6, Romans 8)
Go forth secure in the knowledge
that you are God's beloved child.
May the strength of this identity enable you to say,
"Here I am, send me!" when God calls.
And may the blessing of God, the three in one,
abide with you always. Amen.

CONTEMPORARY OPTIONS

Contemporary Gathering Words (Romans 8, John 3)
Do you know you are a child of God?
Come and hear the good news of God's love for you
and for everyone.
We're all Spirit-led and Spirit-born.
How excellent is that?

—OR—

Contemporary Gathering Words
Have you heard the good news?
God has adopted us as sons and daughters.
What a cool identity!
We are Spirit-led and Spirit-born.
**That will give us the strength
to live our lives with joy.**
Come! Let's praise this wonderful God.

Praise Sentences (Psalm 29)
God is strong and thunderously glorious!
God's voice is powerful and full of majesty!
God's voice flashes with fire and thunder!
May God give strength to God's people.
May God bless the people with peace.

JUNE 10, 2012

Second Sunday after Pentecost
Mary J. Scifres

COLOR
Green

SCRIPTURE READINGS
1 Samuel 8:4-20 (11:14-15); Psalm 138; 2 Corinthians 4:13–
5:1; Mark 3:20-35

THEME IDEAS
Building something that lasts is not all it's cracked up to
be. The Israelites want to build a kingdom, complete with
a monarch, but God yearns to be their only ruler and king.
Jesus' mother and siblings want to protect Jesus within
the family, but Jesus yearns to minister to the world, inviting all who would follow Christ into the family.
Corinthian Christians struggled with earthly bodies that
age and decline, but Paul yearns for Christ's followers to
strive for that temple of faith that will last unto eternity.
Building families, creating political structures, and devel-
oping healthy bodies are all worthy goals. Yet today's
scriptures remind us that the call of Christ often leads to
different goals: inclusion and diversity, humility and part-
nership, spirituality and faith. God calls us to build things
that truly last, to build structures that welcome one and
all, and to provide foundations and shelter for all of
creation.

INVITATION AND GATHERING

Call to Worship (1 Samuel 8, Psalm 127, 2 Corinthians 4–5, Mark 3)

Unless God builds our house,
the house is built in vain.
Unless Christ binds us together,
our fellowship will never be a family of faith.
Unless the Spirit blows through our lives,
**the glory and worship we give to the Holy One
is empty and hollow.**
Unless...

Opening Prayer (1 Samuel 8, 2 Corinthians 4–5, Mark 3)

Mother Father God,
bind us together as your family.
Swing wide the doors of our hearts
and the doors of our church,
that we may welcome the stranger in.
Give us a spirit of faith,
that we may be your temples upon this earth,
lovers of your law and givers of your grace.
In Christ's name, we pray. Amen.

PROCLAMATION AND RESPONSE

Prayer of Confession (1 Samuel 8, 2 Corinthians 4–5, Mark 3)

O God our King and our Maker,
forgive us when we try to make you in our image;
forgive us when we turn to earthly rulers
for the wisdom and strength
you have already shown us.
Fulfill your purpose in us,
that we may be your people,
your temples upon this earth,
your sisters and brothers in love and mercy.
In trust and hope, we pray. Amen.

Words of Assurance (Psalm 138, Mark 3)
Even the Most High God regards the lowly
with love and compassion.
Even the perfect Christ welcomes the sinful and lost
with open arms.
Come, we are the brothers and sisters of Christ.
All are forgiven by grace.
We are the family of God.
Praise be for forgiveness in Christ's love!

Passing the Peace of Christ (Mark 3)
We are the family of God. Let us share signs of familial
love and compassion, peace and forgiveness, as we share
in the passing of Christ's peace.

*Response to the Word (Psalm 138, 2 Corinthians 4–5,
Mark 3)*
When the things of this world are wasting away,
do not lose heart.
When we face division, war, and destruction,
do not lose heart.
When our family on earth scatters to the winds,
do not lose heart.
Come to God's temple and rest in Christ's grace,
for God's love endures forever,
and Christ's grace is sufficient for all.

THANKSGIVING AND COMMUNION

Invitation to the Offering (Psalm 138, Mark 3)
Come into God's courts with thanksgiving and praise.
Come offer the strength of your soul and the generosity
of your spirit, that all may know that Christ is our brother
and that we are God's family. All are welcome here.

Offering Prayer (Psalm 138, Mark 3)
We bow before you
with these offerings and gifts,
that you may know our love.

Lift us up,
>that we may see a king
>>who would give his very life for us,
>>>a master who would be a servant,
>>>a savior who would be a friend.
Gather these gifts, and gather your people,
>that we may be your family upon this earth.

SENDING FORTH

Benediction (2 Corinthians 4–5, Mark 3)
Sisters and brothers of Christ, go into all the world!
Go forth with forgiveness and grace.
Go forth with compassion and love.
We go as Christ's family
for all the world to see.

CONTEMPORARY OPTIONS

Contemporary Gathering Words (1 Samuel 8, 11;
2 Corinthians 4–5; Mark 3)
We look to the rulers of this earth
>for leadership, wisdom, and strength.
We look to these bodies of ours
>for stability, fulfillment, and joy.
We look to families and friends
>for love, compassion, and hope.
When rulers betray, when bodies fail,
>and when families disappoint,
>God offers another look.
God will guide us.
God's Spirit will sustain us.
Christ will welcome us home.
Come, my sisters and brothers,
>we are all God's family now.

Praise Sentences (Psalm 138)
Sing of the ways of God.
Praise God for Christ's glorious love!

Give thanks for this steadfast love.
We worship with gratitude and joy!

—*OR*—

Praise Sentences (Psalm 138)
Give thanks to the Lord, for God is good.
This love endures forever!
Give thanks to the Lord, for God is good.
This love endures forever!

JUNE 17, 2012

Third Sunday after Pentecost / Father's Day
Peter Bankson

COLOR
Green

SCRIPTURE READINGS
1 Samuel 15:34–16:13; Psalm 20; 2 Corinthians 5:6-10 (11-13), 14-17; Mark 4:26-34

THEME IDEAS
God's call is often unexpected. In this week's lessons, God interrupts Samuel on his way to Ramah, calling him to go to the house of Jesse, in Bethlehem. While there, God has him anoint David, the youngest child of Jesse, to lead the people. Throughout the readings for this week, the people and their leaders pray for the protection, wisdom, justice, and compassion they need to live by faith. The realm of God is like a mustard seed, tiny as it is planted, but growing mysteriously into something large enough to offer refuge to everyone. We're called to embrace and nurture life in ways we do not understand. Life is a mystery, and we walk by faith.

INVITATION AND GATHERING
Call to Worship (Psalm 72, 2 Corinthians 5)
The Holy One, defender of the poor and needy,
calls us to gather now.

We come, thankful to be a part
of this family of faith.
God knows us well and calls us by name.
**We hear our name and respond to God's call.
The love of Christ urges us on.**

—OR—

Call to Worship (1 Samuel 15, 2 Corinthians 5)

God interrupted Samuel with an unexpected call.
"Here I am, Lord. Send me!"
God surprised Jesse, choosing his youngest son,
David, to be king.
"Here I am, Lord. Send me!"
We join with Christ and are a part
of God's new creation.
O Mighty God, we come to join the harvest.
Gather us in, O Holy One,
for we would be your people.
Amen.

Opening Prayer (2 Corinthians 5)

God of every thought and reality,
    the holy, prophetic sustainer of community,
        we gather here today as your people,
            children of the good news.
Assure us of your presence once again,
    that we may trust the mystery of life and growth,
    as we gather in the name of our Savior,
        who is Jesus, the Christ.

PROCLAMATION AND RESPONSE

Prayer of Confession (Samuel 15, 2 Corinthians 5)

Holy God, you call us to live in mystery,
to walk by faith.
**Yet we long for plans with goals and schedules.
It's hard to live by faith.**

You call us to place our trust in you,
to live according to your direction.
   Yet we want life to make sense
   from a human point of view.
   It's hard to live by faith.
You call us to feel the mystery of life,
to marvel at the power of your love.
   Yet it's not easy to accept your promise
   that everything old has passed away.
   It's hard to live by faith.
Forgive us, holy maker of reality.
   Forgive us for playing god
   instead of accepting our humanity.

Words of Assurance (Mark 4, Psalm 72)
Fear not, for our creator,
   the loving maker of all reality,
   forgives us, and redeems us from violence
   and oppression.
God sows the good news in tiny seeds,
   inviting us to tend the soil of community,
   and marvel as they grow.
In the name of Jesus, who is the Christ,
   you are forgiven.
   In the name of Christ, you are forgiven. Amen.

Passing the Peace of Christ (1 Samuel 15, 2 Corinthians 5)
God calls us in surprising ways,
inviting us into a new creation.
Share the good news with one another:
The peace of Christ is with you.
   The peace of Christ is with you.

Prayer of Preparation (1 Samuel 15, Mark 4)
Holy God, we want to be like Samuel,
      ready to change course when you call,
      ready to do our part
         even when it isn't quite what we expect.

O glorious Spirit of Surprise,
    open our hearts to your word
        in fresh, new ways. Amen.

Response to the Word (1 Samuel 15, 2 Corinthians 5)
Powerful, compassionate giver of mystery,
    grant us the courage to say "yes"
        to your unexpected call,
    and the strength to claim our place with Christ
        in the new creation you are cultivating. Amen.

THANKSGIVING AND COMMUNION

Invitation to the Offering (Mark 4)
These summer days, the earth produces of itself, first
the stalk and then the full grain. We celebrate the abundance of our loving God, and offer up a part of that
abundance now.

Offering Prayer
Holy God,
    magnificent, sustaining farmer of the future,
        receive these gifts, we pray.
Through our offering,
    help us know in some surprising way
        that you are bringing into being
            something wonderful and new. Amen.

Invitation to Communion (2 Corinthians 5, Mark 4)
Holy God, we thank you for the promise
of your presence.
    You call us to be part of your new creation.
Loving Christ, we celebrate your call
to join you in God's new creation.
    We come to join the harvest, to help carry
    your good news out into the world.
Empowering Holy Spirit, we give thanks
that you encourage us to respond with joy.
    Come fill us now, as we gather to share
    your presence in the bread and cup.

SENDING FORTH

Benediction (2 Corinthians 5)
Life is a mystery. We walk by faith.
God calls us when we least expect it,
inviting us to be in Christ.
Walk out into the world, knowing that you are part
of God's life-giving new creation.
Life is a mystery. We walk by faith.
Amen.

CONTEMPORARY OPTIONS

Contemporary Gathering Words (1 Samuel 15)
We come to hear God's call.
Life is a mystery.
We are surprised by what we hear.
We walk by faith.
We are invited to be part of God's new creation.
Life is a mystery. We walk by faith.

Praise Sentences (2 Corinthians 5)
Praise the One who gives us faith.
Praise the One who walks with us.
Praise the One who shrouds life in mystery.
Praise God.
Praise God.
Praise God.

JUNE 24, 2012

Fourth Sunday after Pentecost

B. J. Beu

COLOR

Green

SCRIPTURE READINGS

1 Samuel 17:(1a, 4-11, 19-23), 32-49; Psalm 9:9-20;
2 Corinthians 6:1-13; Mark 4:35-41

THEME IDEAS

God is on the side of the oppressed and defenseless, defending the powerless and lifting up the downtrodden.
While the Hebrew Scripture readings portray God's vindication through earthly violence and military might, the
Epistle speaks of overcoming evil through weapons of
righteousness. The Gospel depicts the one who carried no
sword having power over the very elements of earth and
water. God's presence in our lives gives us the courage to
face danger and overcome our fears.

INVITATION AND GATHERING

Call to Worship (Mark 4)

Waves of despair wash over us.
  Call on the Lord and find peace.
Troubles gather around us.
  Call on the Lord and find safety.

Cares of doubt overwhelm us.
Call on the Lord and find faith.

Opening Prayer (Mark 4)

Lord of wind and sea,
  we turn to you
    when the storms of life
      threaten to overwhelm us;
  we cry out to you in our need
    when the howling winds
      threaten to sweep us away.
Give us your peace, Mighty One,
  and silence the fears within our troubled hearts,
  that we may find our quiet center
    and find strength for the journey. Amen.

PROCLAMATION AND RESPONSE

Prayer of Confession (1 Samuel 17, 2 Corinthians 2, Mark 4)

God of power and might,
  our fears are greater than our foes.
Like the Hebrews facing Goliath,
  we are convinced that we will be destroyed
    if we stand up for what we believe.
Teach us that the weapons of righteousness
  are far stronger than the weapons
    of violence and war.
Help us see that purity, knowledge, patience,
  kindness and genuine love
    are stronger than the forces set against us.
We ask this in the name of the one
  with the strength to turn the other cheek
    and the power to calm the waters
      with a single word: "Peace!" Amen.

Words of Assurance (Mark 4)

Even the waters obey Christ's command.
The one who brings peace to the seas

will bring peace to our lives as well.
Be at peace, your sins are forgiven.

Response to the Word
Not through might and not through power,
  but by Spirit alone, O God,
  shall your people live in peace.
Make us a people of Spirit, O God. Amen.

THANKSGIVING AND COMMUNION

Offering Prayer (1 Samuel 17, Psalm 9)
Merciful God,
  you watch over us
    as a shepherd watches over the flock;
    you care for us and save us
      from those who would harm us.
As sheep of your fold,
  receive our thanks and gratitude
    as we share your gifts
      with a weak and weary world. Amen.

SENDING FORTH

Benediction (1 Samuel 17, Mark 4)
God gives strength to the weak
and courage to the timid.
  **The Lord brings peace to the fearful
  and faith to the doubting,**
Go forth to share God's peace with the world.

CONTEMPORARY OPTIONS

Contemporary Gathering Words (Mark 4)
Storms threaten.
  In Christ, we rest in peace.
Waves crash.
  In Christ, we fear no evil.
Thunder booms.
  In Christ, we find our strength.

Praise Sentences (Psalm 9, Mark 4, 2 Corinthians 6)
Rejoice and sing God's praises.
Our God is an awesome God.
Trust God in times of trial.
Our God is an awesome God.
Rejoice and sing God's praises.
Our God is an awesome God.

JULY 1, 2012

Fifth Sunday after Pentecost
Mary J. Scifres

COLOR
Green

SCRIPTURE READINGS
2 Samuel 1:1, 17-27; Psalm 130; 2 Corinthians 8:7-15;
Mark 5:21-43

THEME IDEAS
Today's New Testament lessons offer a stewardship em-
phasis: giving of ourselves from the gifts and abundance
we have been given. Paul wrote about this important
value to the church at Corinth; and Jesus exemplifies a
similar understanding of giving in today's two stories of
healing. When an important synagogue leader comes to
Jesus, Jesus denies him first priority, instead turning to the
unknown, unclean woman who has touched him and received healing through her own initiative. "Daughter,
your faith has made you well" (v. 34) has become a much-
loved phrase to Christians today. We are challenged to remember, however, that taking initiative to heal and be
healed is now our calling, not just a beloved phrase. Jesus
does not rest after healing this woman, but turns to the
need of the leader's daughter and brings miraculous
life and renewed hope to that troubled household. Simi-
larly, as Christian disciples, we are called to offer hope to

a troubled world by giving freely and abundantly. Alternately, a service of grief and remembrance may be developed today in relation to 2 Samuel 1 and Mark 5:35-43. This is particularly appropriate in a community suffering from the ravages of war or disaster and could be tied, with care, to the upcoming U.S. remembrance of Independence Day.

INVITATION AND GATHERING

Call to Worship (Psalm 130, Mark 5)

Hope in the God of life!
Trust in the God of the ages.
Believe in the Christ of love.
Trust in the Christ of healing.
Come, let your faith bring hope and wholeness!

Opening Prayer (2 Corinthians 8, Mark 5)

God of generous abundance,
    you give us so much of yourself.
For Christ's grace and love,
    for the Spirit's constant presence,
    and for the gifts you have entrusted to us,
        we give you thanks and praise.
As we worship this day,
    reveal your gifts in us.
Remind us of your abundance.
Strengthen our resolve to live
    as the community of faith
        you would have us be.

PROCLAMATION AND RESPONSE

Prayer of Confession (Psalm 130, 2 Corinthians 8, Mark 5)

Healer and Giver of Life,
    we come to you bent down
        with the poverty of our mistakes.
The emptiness of dreams unfulfilled blurs our vision.
The sorrow of sins committed burdens our souls.

The works not completed and the gifts not shared
  haunt our lives.
Forgive us and renew us, gracious God.
Heal us, and make us whole.

Words of Assurance (Mark 5)
  Daughters and sons of God,
    your faith has made you well.
  Go in peace, as forgiven and beloved children of God!

Passing the Peace of Christ (2 Corinthians 8, Mark 5)
  Stop and pay heed. Turn and notice. Reach out and touch.
  We are surrounded by neighbors in need of healing and
  hope. Let us share the gentle touch of grace, signs of peace
  and love.

Response to the Word (2 Corinthians 8, Mark 5)
  May we excel in faith, in speech, and in knowledge.
  May we be eager to give and to share.
  May we be rich in generosity, compassion, and love.
  May we offer healing and hope
  that others may live.

THANKSGIVING AND COMMUNION

Invitation to the Offering (2 Corinthians 8, Mark 5)
  Our Lord Jesus Christ, though he was rich, became poor
  that we might become rich. May we be rich in generosity,
  that others may have enough. May we be rich in compassion, that others may find forgiveness and love. May we
  be rich in our sharing, that others may know faith, hope,
  and healing through the ministries we perform and the
  ministries we support.

Offering Prayer (2 Corinthians 8, Mark 5)
  Generous God,
    grant us life's necessities,
    but not too many luxuries.
  Out of our abundance,
    help us share generously and freely.

Out of our poverty,
    help us receive gracefully and freely.
Like a mighty flame of power and hope,
    rush through our lives and through these gifts,
        that others may know the blessing
            of your healing and hope.

Communion Prayer (2 Corinthians 8)
Pour out your Holy Spirit
    on all of us gathered here,
    and on these gifts of bread and wine.
Make them be for us
    the nourishment of compassion and grace,
    that we may be generous givers
        of mercy and love.
As you have become poor for us,
    giving us your very life,
    help us to be generous to the world,
        that others may live.
By your Spirit,
    make us one with Christ,
    one with each other in giving and grace,
    and one in ministry to a world
        in need of your love,
            until Christ comes in final victory,
                and we feast at the heavenly banquet.
Through Jesus Christ,
    with the Holy Spirit in your holy Church,
    all honor and glory is yours, almighty God,
        now and forevermore.
    Amen.

Benediction (2 Corinthians 8, Mark 5)
Go in confidence and hope.
Your faith has made you well.
    We go in compassion and love.
    Christ's generosity makes it so.
Go in peace to serve God.
    We go to be Christ for a hurting world.

CONTEMPORARY OPTIONS

Contemporary Gathering Words (2 Corinthians 8, Philippians 4:13)
Your faith is strong in the Lord.
You've got to be kidding, right?
You excel in knowledge and speech.
You've got to be kidding, right?
God calls you to finish all that you've started.
You've got to be kidding, right?
Christ trusts you to give all that you have.
You've got to be kidding, right?
The church at Corinth heard these words from Paul and thought,
"You've got to be kidding, right?"
But Paul was no jokester, and God is not kidding.
We are able to do all things through Christ
who strengthens us.

—OR—

Contemporary Gathering Words (2 Corinthians 8, Mark 5)
In truth and courage, God calls.
In trust and hope, Christ speaks.
Listen, believe, trust, hope . . .
We are given great abundance
    to share with a world in need.
Let us worship, that God's reassurance may be ours.

—OR—

Contemporary Gathering Words (Mark 5)
My friends, our faith has made us well.
Our faith is making us well.
Our faith will make us well,
    for we all are God's children now.

Praise Sentences (Psalm 130, Mark 5)
Hope in the God of love!
Hope in the God of love!
Trust in the healing power of Christ!
Trust in the healing power of Christ!

JULY 8, 2012

Sixth Sunday after Pentecost
B. J. Beu

COLOR
Green

SCRIPTURE READINGS
2 Samuel 5:1-5, 9-10; Psalm 48; 2 Corinthians 12:2-10; Mark 6:1-13

THEME IDEAS
What do we really need in life? The readings from the Hebrew Scriptures suggest that we need a mighty warrior to defend us and highly fortified cities to inspire fear in our adversaries. The Epistle and Gospel readings, meanwhile, suggest that true power is made perfect in weakness. We are to take nothing for the journey as we spread the good news and proclaim repentance in Christ's name. If we claim to be followers of Christ, can we really put our faith in worldly might? The scriptures warn us that our ministries will not always be received. Yet we are to press on, shaking off the dust as we travel to those who will receive the gifts we bring in Christ's name.

INVITATION AND GATHERING

Call to Worship (Psalm 48, Mark 6)
Great is the Lord and greatly to be praised.
  Let us take off our shoes,
  for we are standing on holy ground.

God's steadfast love endures forever.
Let us put our trust in God,
taking nothing for the journey
but our faith in Christ.
Come! Let us worship God, our guide and guardian.
Let us worship the Lord.

Opening Prayer (2 Corinthians 12, Mark 6)
Holy God,
remind us again
that your grace is sufficient for our needs,
your power is made perfect in weakness;
teach us to put our trust in you
rather than in our own wealth and cleverness.
As we receive your word this day,
fill our hearts with joy,
fill our bodies with strength for the journey,
and fill our spirits with passion and purpose,
in the name of the one
who sent us into the world
to bring your kingdom here on earth. Amen.

PROCLAMATION AND RESPONSE

Prayer of Confession (2 Corinthians 12, Mark 6)
God above us, God below us, God beside us,
God before us, God behind us, God within us,
God beyond us,
your ways are as beyond us
as the farthest star in the heavens,
yet you are nearer to us
than our very breath.
We seek to be powerful and strong,
but your strength is made perfect
in our weakness.
Forgive our need to set our own course,
to determine our own fate.

Mold us into faithful disciples
    and help us trust that we have what we need,
    even as you send us forth
        with nothing for the journey.
For the sake of Christ, make us weak,
    that we may be strong in your Spirit. Amen.

Words of Assurance (2 Corinthians 12)
God's grace is sufficient for all our needs,
    and is made perfect in weakness.
God's power is within us, guiding us,
    remaking us, completing us,
    reconciling us to one another.
This is good news indeed!

Response to the Word or Benediction (Mark 6)
Christ sends us out with everything we need to build the
kingdom—with nothing but God's presence and the
promise to be with us each and every step of the way. God
sends us forth to heal the world. Amen.

THANKSGIVING AND COMMUNION

Offering Prayer (2 Samuel 5, Mark 6)
Loving Christ,
    you have given us the full measure
        of your wisdom, power, and call to ministry;
    you have been our shepherd
        and guided us to safe pastures and green fields.
Receive our love and commitment
    in this morning's offering.
Use our gifts,
    that the world may know
        the blessings of the living God. Amen.

SENDING FORTH

Benediction (Psalm 48, Mark 6)
God is our guide and guardian.
We fear no evil.

Christ shows us the way.
We need nothing for the journey.
The Spirit gives us power to heal and anoint.
We go forth with the power of God.
Go with God.

CONTEMPORARY OPTIONS

Contemporary Gathering Words (Psalm 48, Mark 6)
God guides our path.
Great is the Lord!
Christ teaches us the way.
Great is the Lord!
The Spirit clothes us with power.
Great is the Lord!
The Holy One leads us to life.
Great is the Lord!

Praise Sentences (Psalm 48)
Great is the Lord and greatly to be praised.
God is our guide and guardian!
Great is the Lord and greatly to be praised.
God brings victory to the pure of heart!
Great is the Lord.
Great is the Lord.
Great is the Lord.

JULY 15, 2012

Seventh Sunday after Pentecost
Leigh Anne Taylor

COLOR
Green

SCRIPTURE READINGS
2 Samuel 6:1-5, 12b-19; Psalm 24; Ephesians 1:3-14;
Mark 6:14-29

THEME IDEAS
The pairing of two dance stories allows us to ponder how
human action can be both sacred and profane, depending
on context and intention. Psalm 24 reminds us that those
with pure intention may come into the presence of God.
The Gospel story of a young girl dancing before Herod for
the head of John the Baptist reminds us that the beauty
and joy of the body can be turned to idolatry. The culmi-
nation of the Epistle lesson, that all who believe may live
for the praise of Christ's glory, points us back to David's
dance before the Lord—to praise God's glory alone.

INVITATION AND GATHERING

Call to Worship (Psalm 24, 2 Samuel 6, Ephesians 1)
The earth is the Lord's!
Everything in creation belongs to God.
   Lift up your eyes!
   See the mighty works of the Lord!

This is the Lord's house! All who hope in the Lord
will be called children of God.
Lift up your hearts!
Receive the gracious gifts of the Lord!
This is the hour for worship and song.
Lift up your voice!
Praise the Lord with all your might!

—OR—

Call to Worship (Ephesians 1)
Hope in Christ!
Hear the word of truth,
the good news of our salvation.
Believe in Christ!
We are sealed with the mark
of the Holy Spirit.
Live in Christ!
We embrace our inheritance,
as children of God.
Live to the glory of Christ!

Opening Prayer (2 Samuel 6, Psalm 24)
God of all creation,
everything that you have made
lifts its unique voice to praise you
in all of your glory.
Even as we worship here,
we join our voices to the one true song—
the song the morning stars began,
the song King David danced,
the song the angels echoed
at the birth of your Son.
Glory to you, Holy God! Glory!
Let this hour of worship
be wholly to the praise of your glory. Amen.

PROCLAMATION AND RESPONSE

Prayer of Confession (Psalm 24)
Holy God,
as we come into the presence
of your divine holiness,
we confess our many shortcomings.
Our hands are not clean;
our actions do not glorify you;
Our hearts are not pure;
our motivations do not glorify you;
Our words are not true;
our deceitfulness does not glorify you;
Our allegiance is fickle;
our idolatry does not glorify you.
By your mercy, O God,
give us hands that are clean,
hearts that are pure,
tongues that are true,
and souls that worship you alone,
that our whole lives may glorify you. Amen.

Words of Assurance (Ephesians 1)
All you who seek God, and who have set your hope
on Jesus Christ, hear the good news:
we have received forgiveness of sins,
according to the riches of God's grace.
As forgiven and beloved children of God,
let us set our hope on Christ,
and live for the praise of his glory.

—OR—

Words of Assurance or Response to the Word (Psalm 24:3-6)
Hear the word of the psalmist:
"Who shall ascend the hill of the LORD?
And who shall stand in [God's] holy place?

Those who have clean hands and pure hearts,
 who do not lift up their souls to what is false,
 and do not swear deceitfully.
They will receive blessing from the LORD,
 and vindication from the God of their salvation.
Such is the company of those who seek [the Lord],
 who seek the face of the God of Jacob."

Response to the Word (Ephesians 1)
This is the word of truth, the gospel of our salvation.
Praise to the glory of Christ.

THANKSGIVING AND COMMUNION

Offering Prayer (Psalm 24, 2 Samuel 6, Ephesians 1)
True God,
 accept our gifts:
 gifts of our lives, our souls, and our treasure.
Multiply and bless these gifts
 and consecrate them to the praise
 of your glory. Amen.

SENDING FORTH

Benediction (2 Samuel 6, Ephesians 1)
Children of God, celebrate the life
 you have been given.
Live your life with all your might,
 as a dance to God's glory.
Live to the praise of God's glory!

CONTEMPORARY OPTIONS

Contemporary Gathering Words (2 Samuel 6)
The Lord is in this house, people of God!
Like King David, let us worship the Lord
 with all our might.
Let us dance our joy,
 unashamed to praise the Lord of the Dance!

Praise Sentences (2 Samuel 6, Ephesians 1)

Dance and shout with all of your might
before the Lord!
Hope in Christ!
Live for the praise of his glory!

JULY 22, 2012

Eighth Sunday after Pentecost

B. J. Beu

COLOR

Green

SCRIPTURE READINGS

2 Samuel 7:1-14a; Psalm 89:20-37; Ephesians 2:11-22;
Mark 6:30-34, 53-56

THEME IDEAS

True kingship and lineage come through shepherding
love and by bringing enemies together in friendship and
kinship, not by keeping them under our feet. The peace
Jesus brought, the peace attested to in both Mark and Ephesians, is not accomplished by force of arms or family lineage, but by the love of a shepherd and by the
reconciliation of enemies. The peace that David brought
through force of arms could not stand—despite God's as-
surances that David's line would last forever. Perhaps
God realized that the peace Israel hoped for by vanquish-
ing its enemies was no real peace.

INVITATION AND GATHERING

Call to Worship (Ephesians 2, Mark 6)

Are you weary from your labors?
Here you will find rest.

We are weary from our work.
Are you burdened by demands of the crowds?
Here you will find peace.
But there are always others who need our help.
Do you seek renewal in fellowship with our shepherd?
Here you will find strength.
We need strength for the journey.
Come to the shepherd and draw courage
from the one who gives us peace.

Opening Prayer (Ephesians 2, Mark 6)
Shepherding God,
lead us in the paths of peace,
that we may lay aside
all hostility within us.
Heal our vision,
that we may see our adversaries
as members of your household
and not as our enemies.
Be our Shepherd,
and we will be the sheep of your pasture,
through Christ Jesus,
our guide and guardian. Amen.

PROCLAMATION AND RESPONSE

Prayer of Confession (Psalm 89, Ephesians 2, Mark 6)
Rock of our salvation,
your love nourishes us
like a spring in the desert.
Even as we yearn for your presence,
we fall back in fear of your holiness,
for your righteousness and justice
bring judgment on our lives.
Like the psalmist before us,
we take you for granted:
as eternal and predictable
as the rising and setting
of the sun and moon.

We shrink at your invitation to find peace,
not through strength of arms,
but through the love of a shepherd
who lays down his life
for the lost sheep of our world.
Heal the hardness of our hearts,
and do not abandon us
when we trust earthly power and might
over a love that heals and brings life.
In the name of our shepherd, amen.

Words of Assurance (Ephesians 2)
In Christ, we are members of the household of God.
In Christ, we become a holy temple,
a dwelling place for the Lord of hosts.
In Christ, we find true forgiveness.

Passing the Peace (Mark 6)
Like the people who walked with Jesus, we are like sheep
without a shepherd. We need a shepherd to guide us and
to give us rest. Come, let us greet one another with signs
of peace as we share our burdens and our joys with the
Lord. Let us share the peace of Christ.

Response to the Word (2 Samuel 7)
Receive the word of the One who abided with the Hebrew
people, traveling in the ark of the covenant containing the
ten commandments. Receive the word of the One who
abides with us still. Be transformed by the words of faith
spoken by God's people since before the kings of old.

THANKSGIVING AND COMMUNION

Offering Prayer (2 Samuel 7, Ephesians 2, Mark 6)
Nurturing God,
before Israel became a great nation,
you shaped your people
and gave them a home;
before you built David a house of cedar,
you gave him rest from the labor
of protecting and defending his people;

before we became part of your household,
you called us to feed in your pasture
and to rest safely in your fields.
In gratitude for your steadfast love,
receive the gifts we bring this day,
that they may be signs of our love
for our shepherd. Amen.

SENDING FORTH

Benediction (Ephesians 2)
The old differences have died away.
In Christ we are one.
The old arguments taste bitter in our mouth.
In Christ we have peace.
The old hatreds have been swallowed up.
In Christ we are whole.
In Christ we know love.

CONTEMPORARY OPTIONS

Contemporary Gathering Words (Mark 6)
We're lost and alone.
Who will be our shepherd?
The Lord is my shepherd.
We're hurt and afraid.
Who will tend our wounds?
The Lord is my shepherd.
We're anxious and confused.
Who will ease our troubled minds?
The Lord is my shepherd.

Praise Sentences (Psalm 89, Mark 6)
Jesus is our shepherd.
Jesus brings us peace.
Jesus is our shepherd
Jesus heals our land!
Jesus is our Shepherd.
Jesus brings us peace.

JULY 29, 2012

Ninth Sunday after Pentecost

Bill Hoppe

COLOR

Green

SCRIPTURE READINGS

2 Samuel 11:1-15; Psalm 14; Ephesians 3:14-21; John 6:1-21

THEME IDEAS

Today's readings are full of apparent contradictions: faith and sin, acceptance and rejection, strength and weakness, fullness and emptiness. Yet every vile deed lamented by the psalmist is offset by God's deliverance. If King David was truly that same psalmist, who could know this truth more intimately than the one who had an infamous affair with Bathsheba? Contrast his loathsome selfishness with the incredible selflessness of Jesus, who transformed a meal sufficient for only a few into a feast for five thousand. This is what Paul speaks of as the redemptive power of God's love, the power to abundantly achieve far more than anything we might ask for or understand.

INVITATION AND GATHERING

Call to Worship (Psalm 14)

Fools say in their hearts, "There is no God."
Too often we have been fools in word or deed.

Still, the Lord looks from heaven
for those who seek God.
**May we be found among the company
of the righteous!**
Deliver us from evil, O God.
Restore your people's fortunes.
Lord, only in you can we find refuge. Amen.

Opening Prayer (Ephesians 3)
Holy One,
we bow our hearts before you this day.
Strengthen us in our innermost being
and dwell in our hearts through faith.
May we be rooted and grounded in Christ,
whose love is beyond all knowledge.
Help us comprehend even the smallest part
of the beautiful mystery of your grace.
Grant that we may experience the fullness
of your presence with us. Amen.

PROCLAMATION AND RESPONSE

Prayer of Confession (Psalm 14)
Who among us hasn't wondered if God really exists?
Who among us hasn't recoiled in revulsion
when reflecting upon the depraved
and loathsome acts we might be capable of?
Who among us hasn't felt the agony
of a life lived apart from God's love?
Yet in our emptiness, in the depths of our despair,
the Lord seeks us out;
the Lord hears our cries;
the Lord becomes our refuge
and our strength.
In you, gentle savior, our hearts are glad;
we rejoice in your salvation.
We pray to you in spirit and in truth. Amen.

Words of Assurance (Ephesians 3)
    The love of God is your firm foundation;
        by faith you are rooted deeply in the Lord.
    May you know the breadth and length
        and height and depth of the love of Christ,
        which surpasses all human knowledge.
    May you attain the fullness of being,
        the fullness of life that God brings.

Response to the Word (Psalm 14, Ephesians 3, John 6)
    Lord, from emptiness, you create substance—
        when we hunger,
            you fill us from your abundance;
        when all seems lost,
            you bring hope and salvation,
            you make possible the impossible.
    We are overcome with joy,
        but we are also terrified of your power.
    Calm and strengthen our hearts
        as we hear your assurance,
            "It is I: Do not be afraid." Amen.

THANKSGIVING AND COMMUNION

Offering Prayer (Psalm 14, Ephesians 3, John 6)
    Gracious Lord,
        you have lavished upon us
            the riches of your glory.
    As Jesus fed the masses, providing enough for all
        with more than enough left over,
            so you have fed us and provided for us.
    You shelter us, care for us,
        and bring us safely to each stop on our journey.
    As you have given to us out of your abundance,
        we return our offering to you
            with praise and thanksgiving.
    In the name of the Savior, we pray. Amen.

SENDING FORTH

Benediction (Ephesians 3)
May you know the richness and fullness
of God's grace.
May you experience every dimension
of the love of Christ.
May the Spirit dwell within you through faith.
To the Holy One, whose power works within us
to accomplish more than we could ask
or imagine or comprehend,
be glory forever and ever! Amen.

CONTEMPORARY OPTIONS

*Contemporary Gathering Words (2 Samuel 11,
Psalm 14, Ephesians 3, John 6)*
When we see what we want, do we simply take it?
How much better to receive a gift freely given.
If our unbridled desires lead us astray, do we admit it?
How much better to bow before our Maker.
Do we know anything? Have we learned anything?
**How much better to know the indescribable
love of God.**

—OR—

*Contemporary Call to Worship (2 Samuel 11, Psalm 14,
Ephesians 3, John 6)*
Holy One,
you have covered the barren places in our lives
with the riches of your grace.
In the agony and emptiness of our sin,
you have filled us with forgiveness.
From a small portion of food,
you have given us sustenance for a lifetime.
Glory and praise to you forever! Amen!

Praise Sentences (Psalm 14)
Praise the Lord, our refuge!
Praise the Lord, our strength!
Praise the Lord, our deliverer!
Praise the Lord! Praise the Lord!

AUGUST 5, 2012

Tenth Sunday after Pentecost
Deborah Sokolove

COLOR
Green

SCRIPTURE READINGS
2 Samuel 11:26–12:13a; Psalm 51:1-12; Ephesians 4:1-16; John 6:24-35

THEME IDEAS
In the reading from 2 Samuel, the prophet confronts David with a parable that leads him to repent of his sin in taking another man's wife. The psalm echoes that repentant mood, begging God to replace guilt with forgiveness, to give the sinner a fresh start and a clean heart. In the letter to the Ephesians, Paul exhorts his readers to see themselves as members of one body, each with differing gifts as they live together in Christ. The Gospel reading contrasts the people's desire for physical miracles with Jesus' reminder that he is the bread of life, God's own gift to the people of God.

INVITATION AND GATHERING

Call to Worship (John 6:35)
Jesus said, "I am the bread of life."
We are hungry for the bread of heaven.

Jesus said, "The bread of God gives life to the world."
We are hungry for eternal life.
Jesus said, "I am the bread of life.
Whoever comes to me will never be hungry,
and whoever believes in me will never be thirsty."
We are here to become what we already are:
the body of Christ, food for a hungry world.

Opening Prayer (Ephesians 4, John 6)
God of forgiveness and new beginnings,
    you feed our hearts with compassion,
    and nourish our souls with the bread of heaven.
As Jesus fed the hungry crowds,
    knowing that they needed both physical bread
        and the bread of heaven,
        fill us with your generous spirit
            and make us one with Christ. Amen.

PROCLAMATION AND RESPONSE

Prayer of Confession (2 Samuel 11–12, Psalm 51, John 6)
Tender, loving God, have mercy on us.
    Like David, we have been greedy,
    grasping for what is not ours
    even though we have enough.
We have forgotten your promise:
that you will fill us with the bread of life.
    Like the crowd that followed Jesus
    to Capernaum, yet did not understand
    what he had given them,
    we seek bread for our bodies
    more than we seek the bread of heaven.
Forget our sins, take away our guilt.
Purge us with hyssop, and we shall be clean.
    Tender, loving God, have mercy on us.

Words of Assurance (Psalm 51)
When we repent, God creates in us a new heart,
and puts a new and right spirit within us.

In the name of Christ, you are forgiven.
In the name of Christ, you are forgiven.
Glory to God. Amen.

Passing the Peace of Christ
Filled with the Spirit of Love and anticipating the heavenly feast, let us exchange signs of peace:
May the peace of Christ be with you always.
May the peace of Christ be with you always.

Response to the Word (2 Samuel 11–12, John 6)
Nourishing Parent of all who hunger,
thank you for opening our hearts and minds
to the gift of your word, the bread of heaven.
Help us hunger for your peace and righteousness
over the things of this world. Amen.

THANKSGIVING AND COMMUNION

Offering Prayer (John 6)
Generous, merciful God,
you invite us to the heavenly feast,
promising to fill us with every good thing.
Bless these ordinary gifts of bread
and fruit of the vine,
that we may be kneaded and pressed
into one holy, living body,
in the name of Christ, who lived and died
and rose again. Amen.

Great Thanksgiving (2 Samuel 11–12, John 6)
Christ be with you.
And also with you.
Lift up your hearts.
We lift them up to God
Let us give our thanks to the Holy One.
It is right to give our thanks and praise.
It is a right, good, and joyful thing
always and everywhere to give our thanks to you,
Author of justice and mercy.

Long ago, your prophet Nathan
   brought your word to David, the king,
   bringing him to repentance
   and renewed love of you.
In your loving kindness,
    you did not cast him away from your presence,
    but restored to him the joy of your salvation.
And so, with your creatures on earth
   and all the heavenly chorus,
   we praise your name
   and join their unending hymn, saying:
   Holy, holy, holy One, God of power and might,
     heaven and earth are full of your glory.
   Hosanna in the highest. Blessed is the one
     who comes in your holy name.
   Hosanna in the highest.
Holy are you, and holy is your child, Jesus Christ.

When the crowds were hungry for miracles,
   he promised that we who come to him
   will never be hungry,
   and we who believe in him
   will never be thirsty.
(*Words of Institution and Memorial Acclamation*)

Pour out your Holy Spirit on us gathered here,
   and on these gifts of bread and wine.
Make them be for us the body and blood of Christ,
   the bread of heaven, broken to feed a hungry world,
   so that we may become one with Christ,
   one with each other, and one in ministry
   to all the world.

Merciful Creator, Bread of Heaven, Spirit of Love,
   we praise your holy, eternal, nameless Name.
   Amen.

SENDING FORTH

Benediction (Ephesians 4)
Go into the world with all humility, gentleness, and patience, bearing with one another in love, in the unity of the Spirit, the bond of peace, and the name of Jesus, who is the Bread of Life.

Amen.

CONTEMPORARY OPTIONS

Contemporary Gathering Words (John 6)
What must we do to perform the works of God?
This is the work of God,
that you believe in the one whom God has sent.

—OR—

Contemporary Gathering Words (John 6)
Jesus said, "I am the bread of life."
We are hungry for the bread of heaven.
Jesus said, "The bread of God gives life to the world."
We are hungry for eternal life.

Praise Sentences (Ephesians 4)
There is one body and one Spirit.
There is one Lord, one faith, one baptism,
one God of all.

AUGUST 12, 2012

Eleventh Sunday after Pentecost
Hans Holznagel

COLOR
Green

SCRIPTURE READINGS
2 Samuel 18:5-29, 15, 31-33; Psalm 130; Ephesians 4:25–5:2; John 6:35, 41-51

THEME IDEAS
In today's readings, the mourner and the complainer each find instruction on facing adversity: blame is rarely the best first reaction. In war, the famously gifted but manipulative king David tries but fails to spare his rebel son. On news of the death, the king pauses, weeping, and instead of lashing out at subordinates, owns responsibility: "Would I had died instead of you, O Absalom" (2 Samuel 18:33). Jesus asks his listeners not to "complain among yourselves" (John 6:43), but to hear carefully his controversial point. The author of Ephesians counsels replacing "evil talk" and "slander" with "what is useful for building up" (4:29-31). If, from the depths, hope is found in waiting (Psalm 130:5), is it sometimes found in waiting…before speaking?

INVITATION AND GATHERING

Call to Worship (Psalm 130)

Out of the depths I cry to you, O God.
**Let your ears be attentive to the voice
of my supplication!**
I wait for you; my soul waits.
**In your word I hope,
more than those who watch for the morning.**
Let us worship God.

Opening Prayer (Ephesians 4)

We come to you, O God,
eager to be refreshed by song, by word,
by the presence of the Holy Spirit
in this gathered community.
Come to us, we pray,
not just to comfort,
but also to challenge us to better lives,
to move us toward your will.
Be with us in this hour. Amen.

PROCLAMATION AND RESPONSE

Prayer of Confession (Psalm 130, Ephesians 4, 2 Samuel 18)

In hard times as in good times,
guide us, O God.
When feelings flare:
among family, friends, or strangers,
cause us to pause, to wait upon you.
Let malice and bitterness
give way to that which builds up.
Even in deep loss,
let anger be healthy, but let it never possess us;
let blame be sparing, and never let it stand.
Grant us words of love
and feed us from the Bread of Life. Amen.

Words of Assurance (Ephesians 4)

Beloved, know that God in Christ has forgiven you.
Therefore be imitators of God as beloved children,
and live in love. Amen.

Response to the Word (Psalm 130)

With God is steadfast love. With God is great power to redeem. May our hope always be in God. Amen.

THANKSGIVING AND COMMUNION

Invitation to the Offering (John 6:35)

Jesus said to them, "I am the bread of life. Whoever comes to me will never be hungry, whoever believes in me will never be thirsty." Let us share, then, of the blessings we have received, that those who hunger and thirst in these days—whether spiritually or physically—may be ministered to in the name of the living Christ. Let us share our tithes and offerings.

Offering Prayer (Ephesians 4)

May these tithes and offerings, O God,
enable ministry through your church
in places of need near and far.
May the very act of giving
be a ministry to us as well,
conditioning our hearts to daily generosity
of word, spirit, and action.
In Jesus' name we pray. Amen.

SENDING FORTH

Benediction (Ephesians 4)

Put away falsehood.
Speak truth to your neighbors.
Do not make room for the devil.
Be kind and tenderhearted, forgiving one another,
as God in Christ has forgiven you.
Go in peace. Amen.

CONTEMPORARY OPTIONS

Contemporary Gathering Words (Psalm 130, Ephesians 4)

Voice. Ears. Soul. Hope.
Truth. Honesty. Grace. Kindness.
With God is the power of love—
    a love to be lived, as Christ has loved us.

—*OR*—

Contemporary Gathering Words (John 6, Ephesians 4, Psalm 130)

Come as you are, people of God.
Whether angry, wrangled, bitter,
    done wrong, tired of waiting . . .
    come, take bread for the soul, the bread of life.
With God is great power to redeem.

Praise Sentences (Psalm 130, John 6)

Hope in God, O people!
With God is steadfast love.
With God is power to redeem:
    drawing us to bread, to life,
    to new manna from above.

AUGUST 19, 2012

Twelfth Sunday after Pentecost
Mary Petrina Boyd

COLOR
Green

SCRIPTURE READINGS
1 Kings 2:10-12; 3:3-14; Psalm 111; Ephesians 5:15-20;
John 6:51-58

THEME IDEAS
God's gift of Wisdom weaves these readings together.
When offered a divine gift, Solomon asks for wisdom, so
that he can govern Israel. Psalm 111 praises God, giving
thanks for all of God's works and proclaiming respect for
God as the source of all wisdom. Ephesians counsels the
reader to live wisely and fathom God's will. In John, Jesus
speaks of himself as the living bread that brings believers
eternal life. Jesus is wisdom, who brings life to the world.

INVITATION AND GATHERING

Call to Worship (Psalm 111)
God's works are great.
   Our delight is in the Lord.
God's works are full of honor and majesty!
   God's righteousness endures forever.
God is gracious and merciful.
   God's works are faithful and just.

God is worthy to be praised.
Praise the Lord!

—OR—

Call to Worship (Psalm 111, Ephesians 5)
Great are God's works!
Holy and awesome is God's name!
Sing songs of praise to God.
Make melody to the Lord.
At all times give thanks.
For all things give thanks.
God is faithful.
Praise the Lord!

Opening Prayer (1 Kings 2, Ephesians 5)
God of wisdom,
  open our hearts to your call.
Give us understanding minds,
  that we may know your will.
Give us discerning minds,
  that we may see your truth
    and walk in paths of righteousness.
Teach us to use our time wisely,
  that we may make good use of your gifts.
Give us joyful hearts,
  that we may sing and rejoice in your love.
Fill us with your Spirit,
  that we may walk in wisdom all our days. Amen.

PROCLAMATION AND RESPONSE

Prayer of Confession (1 Kings 2, John 6, Ephesians)
Caring God,
    when you ask, "What shall I give you?"
      we ask for creature comforts and an easy life;
    when you offer us wisdom,
      we chase after our own desires.

187

We misuse your precious gift of time,
   pursuing foolish things.
We forget that you are the true bread
   that nourishes our souls.
Teach us your ways of wisdom,
   that we may discern what is good.
Give us wise hearts,
   that we may turn to you and find our way.
Feed us with the bread of life,
   that we may walk in faithfulness before you. Amen.

Words of Assurance (Psalm 111)
God's love is steadfast and faithful.
God is gracious and merciful.
In God, we are a forgiven people.

Passing the Peace of Christ (John 6)
Christ is the living bread, feeding our souls.
Christ is the wisdom of God, nourishing our minds.
Christ is the world's peace, calling us all to love.

Response to the Word (1 Kings 2)
Gracious God,
   you offer humanity a choice:
      we will walk in your ways—
         the ways of wisdom and goodness,
         the ways of justice and righteousness,
      or will we live as unwise people,
         turning aside from your gracious mercy.
Give us wise and discerning minds,
   that we may be faithful to you in all that we do.
Lead our feet on your paths
   of righteousness and justice.
Teach us your peace. Amen.

THANKSGIVING AND COMMUNION

Invitation to the Offering (1 Kings 2–3, Psalm 111)
God's ways lead to a rich and meaningful life. God's paths
lead to righteousness and justice and abundant resources.

Choose God's ways of wisdom and bring your gifts, that
God's works may flourish in our world.

Offering Prayer (Psalm 111)

Wise and loving God,
    you have given us a heritage of faith,
    you show us the ways of wisdom
        that lead to life and peace.
We are rich in your blessings.
With grateful hearts,
    we offer you our gifts,
        that they may enable your work
            of justice and mercy;
    we offer you our very selves,
        that we may walk in your ways
            of understanding and wisdom. Amen.

Great Thanksgiving (1 Kings 2–3, Psalm 111, John 6)

Source of wisdom, giver of life,
    we thank you for the abundance of your love.
Your works reflect your glory,
    from the great galaxies whirling in space,
    to the tiniest ant, hard at work in the soil.
You feed us and teach us your ways.
From generation to generation
    you offer your people steadfast love.
You are gracious and merciful,
    calling us back to you with a forgiving love.
You are faithful and just,
    hearing the cries of those who are oppressed,
    leading us on paths of righteousness.
Your love is great,
    and we praise your awesome name.
(Sanctus)

You sent Jesus to walk beside us,
    showing us your ways of wisdom.
He taught your ways of justice and truth.

He led us toward you,
    showing us what is good,
    helping us understand your ways.
He came among us,
    offering himself in love.
Jesus is the living bread,
    the hope of the world,
    the promise of eternal grace.

On his last night,
    Jesus gathered with his followers at a meal.
He gave thanks to you with his whole heart,
    took bread, broke it,
    and offered it to his followers, saying:
    "I am the living bread
    that came down from heaven."
As we eat this bread, we taste eternity.
After the meal, Jesus took a cup,
    filled with the wine of the new covenant.
Again he gave thanks
    and shared it with his followers, saying:
    "This cup is my life,
    the true drink that quenches a deep thirst."
As we drink this cup, we abide in Christ.
Jesus said, "As you eat, and as you drink,
    and as you live—remember me."
Jesus is the source of goodness, the bread of life,
    the true drink, feeding the world's hunger,
    and quenching the world's thirst.
We praise God's awesome name
    and proclaim the mystery of faith:
    Christ has died.
    Christ is risen.
    Christ will come again.

Pour out your Holy Spirit on us gathered here,
    that we may be filled with your Spirit,

transformed by your word,
and born anew in your love.
Send your Spirit on these gifts—
wheat from the fields, grapes from the vine—
that they may become for us
the living presence of Christ,
true food and true drink,
bringing life to the world.
Praise to you, God of Wisdom.
Praise to you, Living Bread.
Praise to you, Spirit of Life.
Praise for all that is good and wise, and wonderful. Amen.

SENDING FORTH

Benediction (1 Kings 2, John 6)
The God of steadfast love blesses you.
Jesus, the living bread, feeds you.
The Spirit of wisdom guides you.
Go forth with delight to walk in God's ways,
rejoicing in God's faithfulness.

CONTEMPORARY OPTIONS

Contemporary Gathering Words (1 Kings 2–3, Psalm 111)
What do you want from God?
We don't know.
Do you want riches and power?
No, we want something more.
Do you want wisdom and peace?
Yes, that will lead us to God!
Praise our God, who gives us wisdom!
Holy and awesome is our God!

—OR—

Contemporary Gathering Words (Ephesians 5)
Let the Spirit fill you.
Let us sing songs together!

Make melody to God in your hearts!
We will rejoice and be glad!
Give thanks to God.
Give thanks to God for everything!

Praise Sentences (Psalm 111)

God's works are great!
Holy and awesome is God's name!
Holy and awesome is our God!
Praise God! Alleluia!

AUGUST 26, 2012

Thirteenth Sunday after Pentecost
Mary J. Scifres

COLOR
Green

SCRIPTURE READINGS
1 Kings 8:(1, 6, 10-11), 22-30, 41-43; Psalm 84;
Ephesians 6:10-20; John 6:56-69

THEME IDEAS
Though God did not want a temple upon this earth,
Solomon built the temple and celebrated the permanent
placement of the Ark of the Covenant. Christ calls us to
lives of love and forgiveness, justice, and peace; yet Paul
writes in images of militaristic might. Jesus speaks of a
new commandment that will overturn the old practice of
ritual sacrifice, yet he speaks of eating his flesh and drink-
ing his blood that we might live. These contradictory images often trouble us as preachers and worship planners.
Yet the paradox of faith is the staple of our diet. Like God's
followers of old, we are challenged to integrate even
wrong choices and wrongdoing into the ongoing journey
of following Christ. Even when the journey leads to death
and the cross, we proclaim resurrection. Let today's contradictions birth new life and new perspectives into our
message and worship.

INVITATION AND GATHERING

Call to Worship (Psalm 84, Ephesians 6)
How lovely, Lord, how lovely
to worship in this holy place.
How lovely, Lord, how lovely
to walk with you all of our days.
How lovely, Lord, how lovely
to live as your people on earth.
How lovely, Lord, how lovely
to be strengthened and blessed by your grace.

Opening Prayer (1 Kings 8, Psalm 84, Ephesians 6)
God of heavenly hosts,
we come before you with songs of praise.
As we gather in this earthly sanctuary,
we are reminded that your presence
is not limited by these walls.
Be with us now and always
as we call upon your name.
Hear our prayers,
and speak to our souls.
Embrace us with the strength of your mighty love,
that we may go forth with our faith emboldened
and our courage strengthened to do your will.

PROCLAMATION AND RESPONSE

Prayer of Confession (1 Kings 8, Ephesians 6)
God of grace and glory,
forgive us when we try to imprison you
in walls that divide and boxes that constrict;
forgive us when we mistake courage
with power over others and envision strength
as something to wield
for our own self-protection.
Open our hearts and our minds
to truly know and comprehend
the mystery of faith.

Embolden us to live with the courage of faith
and the strength of steadfast love.
Transform us into your temples upon this earth,
that you might live in our hearts
and in our every footstep.
In Christ's name, we pray. Amen.

Words of Assurance (Psalm 84, Ephesians 6)
Happy are those whose strength is in God.
Happy are those who trust in Christ's love.
Rest in God's might and believe in Christ's love,
for all are forgiven in Christ.

Passing the Peace of Christ (Ephesians 6)
Paul guides us to wear whatever it takes to be ready to
proclaim the gospel of peace. Let us wear our faith well as
we offer signs of peace to one another, that all may be
ready to share Christ's gospel of peace with a hurting
world.

Response to the Word or Benediction (Ephesians 6)
Be strong in God's wisdom and power.
May our armor be compassion and love.
Stand firm in truth and faith.
May our shields reflect Christ's glory.
Pray for salvation and righteousness.
May our sword be the beacon of the Spirit.
Proclaim the gospel of peace.
Our feet are ready to go forth in love.

THANKSGIVING AND COMMUNION

Invitation to the Offering (1 Kings 8, Ephesians 6)
Into this holy place we have come to worship and praise,
to listen and learn. Know that God is not contained here,
for God is the Lord of all. Christ yearns to fling open the
doors and spring forth with God's gospel of love and
peace. Let us share of ourselves through the gifts that we
give and the lives that we live.

Offering Prayer (1 Kings 8, Matthew 6, Luke 11)
We offer these gifts to you, God of heaven and earth,
that a bit of your heavenly presence
may touch the peoples of this earth.
Through our offerings,
may your realm come;
may your will be done
on earth as it is in heaven. Amen.

Invitation to Communion (John 6)
Come to Christ, the bread of life.
Come to Christ's table now.
Drink of God's love, the spring of eternity.
Come to Christ's table now.

Words of Blessing (John 6)
Take and eat. This is the bread of life that never ends.
Take and drink. This is the cup of love
that flows through us.
Abide in Christ, and Christ will abide in you.

SENDING FORTH

Benediction (Ephesians 6)
Go forth with the strength of God.
We go with God's mighty faith and hope.
Go forth with the boldness of Christ.
We go with Christ's courageous peace and love.

CONTEMPORARY OPTIONS

Contemporary Gathering Words (1 Kings 8, Psalm 84, Ephesians 6)
Come to God's temple, put on Christ's armor.
Temples and armor? These are not for us!
Temples of salvation, sanctuaries of peace…
these are the sacred places God desires.
What else should we wear?

A belt of truth, a shield of faith,
and a gospel of love... this is the armor of Christ.
We will wear the Lord's clothing.
Come to God's temple of peace
and put on Christ's armor of love.
We come with praise and joy!

Praise Sentences (Psalm 84, John 6)
Happy are those who trust in Christ!
With joy, we sing to the living God!
Happy are those who trust in Christ!
With joy, we sing to the living God!

SEPTEMBER 2, 2012

Fourteenth Sunday after Pentecost

B. J. Beu

COLOR
Green

SCRIPTURE READINGS
Song of Solomon 2:8-13; Psalm 45:1-2, 6-9 (or Psalm 72); James 1:17-27; Mark 7:1-8, 14-15, 21-23

THEME IDEAS
In luscious imagery and aromatic detail, the Song of Solomon and Psalm 42 depict the joy to be found in union with our loving God. Delicious fruit and oils of gladness image a joyous world—the world as God intends. How quickly this world descends into malicious gossip and sniping about eating with defiled hands. The Epistle warns us against hearing the word without living the word, and the Gospel warns us against confusing human convention with divine instruction.

INVITATION AND GATHERING

Call to Worship (Song of Solomon 2, Psalm 45)
The voice of God calls:
"Arise, my fair one, and come away."
Love comes to us with joy,
beckoning us to leave behind
the winter of our lives.

The voice of God calls:
"Smell the flowers, taste the fruit of the vine."
Oils of gladness fill our senses
with peace and contentment.
Beautiful instruments sound with your glory.
The voice of God calls:
"Arise, my fair one, and come away."
Love comes to us this morning.

Opening Prayer (Song of Solomon 2, Psalm 45)
Bountiful God,
your presence stirs the heart
like oils of gladness—
sweet-smelling frankincense,
sandalwood, myrrh, and pungent cassia;
your voice delights the mind
like the fragrance of wild flowers
and the blossoms of spring.
As the fruit of the vine
gladdens our hearts,
so your call gladdens our spirits.
Call us to you once more,
that we may hearken to the voice
of our beloved. Amen.

PROCLAMATION AND RESPONSE

Prayer of Confession (James 1, Mark 7)
Life-giving God,
it is so easy to confuse our righteous indignation
for the true demands of your justice;
it is so easy to assume our anger is your anger.
Forgive us when our unbridled tongues speak evil
and render our religious fervor
worthless in your eyes.
Teach us the difference
between our human precepts
and your life-giving word.

Help us to be doers of your word,
    that we may be disciples
        in more than name alone. Amen.

Words of Assurance (Psalm 45, James 1)
God's throne endures forever.
God's might brings equity to the earth.
The One who calls us and anoints our life
    will fill us with joy and bring us fullness of grace.

Passing the Peace of Christ (Song of Solomon 2)
The peace of Christ is more wonderful than the oils of
gladness. Share this peace with those around you as we
greet one another in Christ's name.

Response to the Word (James 1:22, 25)
Let us be doers of the word and not hearers only. For those
who look into the perfect law, the law of liberty, and per-
severe, being not hearers who forget but doers who act—
they will be blessed in their doing. So may it be for us.

THANKSGIVING AND COMMUNION

Offering Prayer (James 1)
God of light,
    every generous act of giving
        and every perfect gift is from you.
As you gave birth to your word of truth,
    that we might bear the first fruit of your Spirit,
    may our offerings be evidence of this harvest,
        to testify to your glory.
In Christ's name we pray. Amen.

SENDING FORTH

Benediction (Song of Solomon 2, Psalm 45, James 1)
God has anointed us with the oils of gladness.
God has blessed us with songs of mirth.
Christ has lit our path with the law of light.
Christ has made us into the family of God.

The Spirit fills our inward being with truth.
The Spirit shows us the way.
Thanks be to God!

CONTEMPORARY OPTIONS

Contemporary Gathering Words (Song of Solomon 2, Psalm 45)

Arise, my beloved, and come away!
We will come with you.
Arise, my beloved, and find beauty.
We rejoice in God's splendor.
Arise, my beloved, and come away!
We will come with you.

Praise Sentences (Song of Solomon 2, Psalm 45)

Our God leaps like a gazelle into the heart!
Our God refreshes the spirit with the oils of gladness.
Bless the Lord, O my soul.
Bless the Lord!

SEPTEMBER 9, 2012

Fifteenth Sunday after Pentecost
June Boutwell

COLOR
Green

SCRIPTURE READINGS
Proverbs 22:1-2, 8-9, 22-23; Psalm 125 (or Psalm 124); James 2:1-10 (11-13), 14-17; Mark 7:24-37

THEME IDEAS
We are to tend to the needs of those around us—the needs of the less fortunate and marginalized. Failure to do so results in godly wrath and calamity. There is a strong distinction in these scriptures between rich and poor, especially in the Epistle lesson. There is a strong theme of God's favor for the poor and a call to live righteously. The Gospel recounts the story of a deaf man healed and a Syrophoenician woman who challenges Jesus to view those outside the Jewish community as worthy of grace and blessing.

INVITATION AND GATHERING

Call to Worship (Proverbs 22:2, 9; Psalm 125:1-2, 4; James 2:5)
Those who trust in God are like the mountains, immovable and abiding.

God shelters the people:
today and for eternity.
Rich or poor, God creates us to pursue justice
and to care for one another.
Be a blessing, O God, to those who are good
and upright in heart.
God calls us to be rich in faith,
to honor our heritage as heirs of the Kingdom.
We are blessed when we share our blessings,
that peace may be upon the people.

Opening Prayer (Psalm 125:3-4; Proverbs 22:1, 17, 21)

Holy One,
we call upon your name,
for we know that your name and favor
are more precious than human riches.
You hate wickedness
and abhor the neglect of your people.
You call us to righteousness,
to reach out to others with justice and mercy.
You teach us right from wrong,
that we may truly live in your grace.
In the shadow of that grace,
we offer compassion and mercy to others.
Abide with us this day,
that we may serve you forevermore. Amen.

PROCLAMATION AND RESPONSE

Prayer of Confession (Psalm 125, Proverbs 22, James 2)

Gracious God,
we come before you today
knowing that we often fall short of your call
to love one another well.
We allow ourselves to be blinded
by wealth and power.
We ignore those around us
who suffer injustice, poverty, and rejection.

We tune out the cries of the poor
   and those on the edges of our communities.
Help us to see your great generosity,
   hear your word of mercy,
      and feel your great love
         for all who need your redemptive grace.
Strengthen us to reach out in service
   to those who are in need.
Make us aware of those outside our own communities,
   that we may see them as your precious children
      and serve them in humility and joy.
May we continue to grow in grace
   as we learn how to serve you
      in the name of the great Servant,
         even Jesus Christ. Amen.

Words of Assurance (1 Corinthians 2:12)
We have received, not the spirit of the world,
   but the Spirit that is from God.
May we understand the grace and forgiveness
   bestowed upon us by God,
      that others may find the Kingdom
      within us and among us.

Passing the Peace of Christ (John 14:3, 21, 27)
Knowing that God has prepared a place for us; knowing that Christ has come to bring us peace, let us greet one another now in the power of God and the glory of Christ's peace.

Response to the Word (James 2:14-17, Psalm 125)
It is easy to be overwhelmed by the pain of the world. We want to turn off the evening news and tune out the stories of human suffering, but God calls us to pay attention to those around us, to do more than simply give to worthy causes, to do more than pray the situation into God's hands. Our faith is to be lived out in righteous actions, that we might resist wickedness and avoid condemnation for our lack of compassion. We are challenged to meet the

needs of others, to reach out with hand and heart, to provide for the real human needs of others.

THANKSGIVING AND COMMUNION

Invitation to the Offering

We who have been richly blessed are called to share that
blessing with the world. Give freely in the joy of serving
your neighbor and your God.

Offering Prayer (Proverbs 22:1-2)

All that we do is in your holy name, O God.
Even as we share the riches of our labors,
may we continue to honor your name
in all that we do.
Bless these gifts given freely,
that your justice and mercy may prevail
in a weak and weary world. Amen.

Invitation to Communion

This table is open to all who recognize Jesus Christ as
healer and redeemer. This table is open to all who work to
bring God's Kingdom here on earth. No one is turned
away because of life circumstances. No one is barred from
this table. No one seeking God's abundant grace and
mercy is turned aside. We see before us the abundance
that a life of faith offers as we respond to God's everlasting mercy in prayer and deed.

The Great Thanksgiving (James 2, Mark 7)

Eternal God, Creator of the heavens and the earth
and all who dwell therein,
we give you thanks for all that surrounds us.
We thank you for making us
but a little lower than the angels,
children of your grace.
We are grateful for your mercy,
forgiving our human pride
and our blindness to those in need.

We rejoice in the hope and salvation
found in the person of Jesus Christ,
who shared our earthly suffering and joy.
We remember Christ's death,
celebrate with joy Christ's resurrection,
and seek to follow in Christ's way,
serving those around us.
In the steadfast comfort of the Holy Spirit,
we offer ourselves to your service
as we unite our voices to glorify you.
**Holy, holy, holy God of love and majesty,
the whole universe speaks of your glory,
O God Most High.
Blessed is the one who comes
in the name of our God!
Hosanna in the highest!**

At this table we recall the night
when Jesus was at table with his friends.
As they were eating, Jesus took bread,
blessed and broke it.
He gave it to the disciples, saying,
"Take, eat. This is my body
which is broken for you.
Do this in remembrance of me."
In the same manner, Jesus also took the cup, saying,
"This cup is the new covenant in my blood.
Do this, as often as you drink it,
in remembrance of me."
By partaking at this table, we proclaim Christ's death,
celebrate Christ's resurrection,
and await Christ's return.

Communion Prayer
Gracious God,
we ask you to bless this bread and cup.
May we be strengthened through your Holy Spirit
to be the body of Christ,

your servant people,
faithful in all things and humble in our service
to you and your people. Amen.

Prayer of Thanksgiving
We give thanks, almighty God,
that you have refreshed us at your table
by granting us the presence of Jesus Christ.
Strengthen our faith,
increase our love for one another,
and send us forth into the world
in courage and peace,
rejoicing in the power of the Holy Spirit,
through Jesus Christ our Savior. Amen.

SENDING FORTH

Benediction (James 2:5, 17)
Go forth to love one another.
Be rich in faith and serve one another
in all joy and humility.
And may the power of God our Creator,
Christ our Salvation,
and the communion of the Holy Spirit
be with us now and forever. Amen.

CONTEMPORARY OPTIONS

Contemporary Gathering Words (James 2, Psalm 125, THE MESSAGE)
Friends, don't let public opinion
influence how you live out your faith.
God lives by different rules.
God lifts up and honors the poor
while sending the rich away empty.
God's favor is promised to those who love God.
Love is more than saying the right words,
it is doing the right thing for others.
Be good to your people, O God.
The hearts of the people are right!

—OR—

Contemporary Gathering Words (Luke 7, Psalm 125, THE MESSAGE)

We can trust God.
   God is like the mountain: rock solid.
God loves all the people:
   the poor, the disabled, the outcast,
   the stranger.
We can depend on God.
   God feeds the hungry, heals the sick,
   and restores relationships.
Praise our Loving God.
   Hallelujah. Hallelujah. Hallelujah.

Praise Sentences

Praise the rock of our faith.
Praise the source of our salvation.
Praise the strength of our hope.
Praise God.
Praise God.
Praise God.
(B. J. Beu)

SEPTEMBER 16, 2012

Sixteenth Sunday after Pentecost
Joanne Carlson Brown

COLOR
Green

SCRIPTURE READINGS
Proverbs 1:20-33; Psalm 19; James 3:1-12; Mark 8:27-38

THEME IDEAS
Words, words, words, words—a collection of letters but what power they have. The readings today all speak to the effects and consequences of what we say, what we proclaim, how we use our tongues. We can praise God, confess Jesus as the Christ, speak words of wisdom—or we can ignore wisdom and speak folly, curse God, and deny the costs of discipleship. What we listen to and what we proclaim makes all the difference in our lives.

INVITATION AND GATHERING

Call to Worship (Proverbs 1, Mark 8)
Wisdom cries out in the streets.
We hear and struggle to understand.
Come and listen to the words of life and love.
We hear and proclaim our faith
in the one who brings life.
Let us worship the God of life and wisdom
whose words guide our life on the right paths.

Opening Prayer (Proverbs 1, Psalm 19, James 3, Mark 8)

Loving and caring God,
    we come this morning
        seeking wisdom and guidance for our lives.
Open us to your words of life and love and truth.
May we proclaim with our tongues
    what we know in our hearts.
In this time of worship,
    help us more fully understand
        what it means to truly be a disciple,
        a follower of the way of Jesus,
        a follower of the path of wisdom.
May the words of our mouths
    and the meditation of our hearts
        be acceptable to you,
            our rock and our redeemer. Amen.

PROCLAMATION AND RESPONSE

Prayer of Confession (Proverbs 1, Psalm 19, James 3, Mark 8)

Wisdom cries in the streets,
    but we do not listen or understand.
The words of your law are spoken,
    but we rarely pay heed or obey.
You call us to declare who Jesus is for us,
    but we can't seem to get the right words out.
Our tongues engage before our brains do.
We want so much to be a people
    who are faithful to your word
        and led by your guidance,
        but we are so easily distracted
            by the cacophony of words and sounds
                that surround us each day.
Forgive us when we are quick to speak
    and slow to understand.

Forgive us when we do not hear your wisdom
    in all the ways you speak to us.
Forgive us when we do not even try
    to truly understand what it means
        to be your disciples.
Lead us back to the path of wisdom and life,
    that we may truly live. Amen.

Words of Assurance (Proverbs 1)

Those who listen to the words of wisdom
    will be secure and live in ease.
Know that our God never ceases
    to reach out in love and forgiveness,
    guiding us on the path of life and righteousness,
    calling us to claim our true identity
    as disciples and beloved sons and daughters
    of the living God.

Prayer of Preparation (Psalm 19)

Let the words of my mouth
    and the meditation of my heart
        be acceptable to you, O God,
            my rock and my redeemer.

Response to the Word (Proverbs 1, Psalm 19, Mark 8)

For the wisdom in your word,
    for your call to faithfulness,
    for your gift of promise,
        we give you thanks.

THANKSGIVING AND COMMUNION

Invitation to the Offering (Proverbs 1, Mark 8)

We are called to listen to the words of wisdom and to respond with our whole lives. Let us give thanks to God with all that we are and all that we have—in word, thought, and action.

Offering Prayer

God, we hear and we respond
    to your words of wisdom.
        your words of call and life.

May these gifts, not only of our money,
   but of our very selves—
      our words, our thoughts, our actions—
         be acceptable to you,
            and help spread your words
               of life and love. Amen.

SENDING FORTH

Benediction (Proverbs 1, Mark 8)
Go forth with the words of wisdom crying in your ears.
Go forth with songs of hope singing in your heart.
Know that you are called to be faithful followers
   of the One who will always be near you,
      will always guide and encourage you
         to walk the path of life. Amen.

CONTEMPORARY OPTIONS

Contemporary Gathering Words
Come from wherever you are
   and hear the words of wisdom
   from our living, loving God.
Listen, rejoice, and follow.

—OR—

Contemporary Gathering Words (Proverbs 1)
Can you hear it?
   What?
Wisdom is crying in the streets.
   What does that have to do with us?
We are called to listen, to respond, and to obey.
   **We'll open our ears and our hearts
   to God's words.**
Come, let us worship the God of wisdom and life.

Praise Sentences (Psalm 19)
The heavens are telling the glory of God!
The law of God revives the soul.
The way of God rejoices the heart.
The word of God endures forever.

SEPTEMBER 23, 2012

Seventeenth Sunday after Pentecost
Mary J. Scifres

COLOR
Green

SCRIPTURE READINGS
Proverbs 31:10-31; Psalm 1; James 3:13–4:3, 7-8a;
Mark 9:30-37

THEME IDEAS
The Lord calls us to godly wisdom and righteous living.
This is not the godliness born of perfect ritual and sacrifice
but rather of goodness and kindness. The wife in
Proverbs, who is "far more precious than jewels" (v. 10), is
the one who speaks with wisdom and teaches kindness,
who is girded in strength and living with purpose. The
psalmist proclaims that happiness comes to those who delight in God's law, who find growth and strength in med-
itating upon, and living in, the wisdom God offers.
Likewise, James explores wisdom as that which results in
gentleness, peace, mercy, and righteousness. This "wisdom from above" is a puzzle to us, no less than it was to
the disciples, as we are tempted to seek greatness in
power over others. In gathering a child into his arms,
Jesus offers a vivid image of true greatness—the greatness
that welcomes a nameless child as a precious gift. In drawing near to God, we discover the wisdom that is from

above and find the powerful strength to follow in Christ's footsteps.

INVITATION AND GATHERING

Call to Worship (Psalm 1, James 4)
Draw near to God, and God will draw near to you.
We seek God's wisdom,
the water of Christ's teachings.
Rest in the shade of this tree called the church.
We yearn for the strength
to move forward in faith.
Plant your hearts in God's truth,
your lives in Christ's ways.
We come now to listen,
to speak, and to pray.
Draw near to God, and God will draw near to you.

Opening Prayer (Proverbs 31, James 3)
Wise and Wonderful One,
speak words of wisdom,
that we might hear and believe.
Instill in us the ways of righteousness
which are far more precious than jewels.
Make us wise and understanding in word and action,
that we may be people of peace and compassion,
bearing the fruit of mercy and love.

PROCLAMATION AND RESPONSE

Prayer of Confession (Proverbs 31, Psalm 1, James 3)
Loving God,
grant us the mercy
you would have us grant to others.
When we seek after the wealth of this world,
forgive our selfish striving.
When we yearn for the power that boosts our pride,
forgive our selfish dreams.

THE ABINGDON WORSHIP ANNUAL 2012

When we plant ourselves in muddy waters,
    lift us onto higher ground
        near fresh streams of living grace.
When we embark on roads
    that lead to destruction and despair,
        guide us onto Christ's path of life.
Loving God,
    grant us your mercy,
        that we in turn may show mercy and compassion
            to all whom we meet.
In hope and gratitude, we pray. Amen.

Words of Assurance (James 4, Mark 9)
Drawing near to God,
    we discover that God has drawn near to us.
Drawing near to Christ,
    we discover that Christ has drawn near to us.
We are all God's children,
    bathed in the waters of righteousness,
    forgiven and welcomed anew!

Passing the Peace of Christ (James 3)
Share the harvest of Christ's righteousness—the gift of
peace for the people of peace. Come, let us share signs of
peace and love.

Response to the Word (Proverbs 31, Psalm 1, James 3)
God's wisdom is ours,
offering strength for the journey.
    **May we walk in God's ways
    on the path of peace.**
Christ's righteousness is ours,
bearing fruit that is pure.
    **May we share Christ's feast
    of kindness and mercy.**
Happy are we when we treasure God
and Christ's ways with a pure heart.
    **Happy are we when God's wisdom lives in us,
    and Christ's love flows through us.**

216

SEPTEMBER 23, 2012

May we be like trees
planted by the living water of Christ.
**May we be streams of mercy
flowing forth with God's love.**

THANKSGIVING AND COMMUNION

Invitation to the Offering (Proverbs 31, James 4)
May we open our hands to the poor and reach out with
love to the needy. May we freely give, that others may
simply live.

Offering Prayer (Psalm 1, James 4)
As we draw near to you, O God,
    draw near to us in these gifts we bring before you.
Bless them with your wisdom and love,
    that through them others may receive
        the gentle touch of your grace
            and the fruit of your life-giving presence.

Invitation to Communion (Psalm 1, Matthew 9)
Come to the table,
    that you may be fed by God's mercy and grace.
Come to the table,
    that you may drink from Christ's stream
    of living water.
Come share in the meal,
    that you may become a tree
    bursting with the fruit of God's love.
Come, children of God, for all are welcome here!

SENDING FORTH

Benediction (James 3, Mark 9)
Go forth as children of God.
Go forth with wisdom and grace.
Go forth with the fruit of Christ's love.
Go forth with the Spirit of peace.
Go forth as children of God.

217

CONTEMPORARY OPTIONS

Contemporary Gathering Words (James 3, James 4, Mark 9)

Wives and husbands, children and parents,
friends and neighbors, enemies and strangers,
draw near to the God of love.
Wise and foolish, compassionate and angry,
loving and kind, disappointed and discouraged,
draw near to the God of love.
Sinners and saints, selfish and generous,
strong and weak, courageous and fearful,
draw near to the God of love.
From all walks of life, as one body
gathered here in Christ's arms of grace,
draw near to the God of love.

Praise Sentences (Proverbs 31, James 3)

Praise God for wisdom and truth!
Praise God for wisdom and truth!
Praise God for strength and love!
Praise God for strength and love!

SEPTEMBER 30, 2012

Eighteenth Sunday after Pentecost
Amy B. Hunter

COLOR

Green

SCRIPTURE READINGS

Esther 7:1-6, 9-10; 9:20-22; Psalm 124; James 5:13-20;
Mark 9:38-50

THEME IDEAS

God is on our side! is a clarion call of the Christian faith, but
one we too often misunderstand to mean that God is our
special possession or the champion of our causes. The
book of Esther tells how God rescues God's people
through the courage and daring of Esther, who finds herself asked to embrace the role of the advocate for her powerless people—even at the risk of losing her life. In Mark's
Gospel, Jesus warns his disciples against believing that
they control access to the power of God. Vying for power
in God's name often leads to abuse of the vulnerable, the
weak, and the powerless. Better to choose personal loss, as
Esther risked, than break the unity of the kingdom of God
through our power plays. Psalm 124 puts it this way: If
we rely on anything other than God, we are lost. God is on
the side of the powerless, calling us to care for and to protect those who are in need.

INVITATION AND GATHERING

Call to Worship (Psalm 124, James 5)
If it had not been God who was on our side,
the troubles of our world
would have swallowed us whole.
If it had not been God who was on our side,
the sorrows of our times
would have swept us away.
Are any among us suffering?
Come and pray.
Are any among us cheerful?
Come sing songs of praise.
Are any among us sick?
Come and ask for healing.
Our help is in our God,
the One who made heaven and earth.
Call upon God, creator and rescuer.
God is on our side.

Opening Prayer (Psalm 124, Mark 9)
Eternal God,
you create us and you rescue us.
Be here with us now.
Help us know how much we need you.
Teach us that no other power can support us
like your power.
As you share your power with us,
teach us to be Christ to the world,
proclaiming your reign for all people.
As you lavish your love upon us,
help us receive that love and offer it to the world,
in Jesus' name. Amen.

PROCLAMATION AND RESPONSE

Prayer of Confession (Esther 7 & 9, Psalm 124, Mark 9)
Creating and rescuing God,
your power amazes us.

Yet even in our amazement,
  we take too long to turn to you,
  forgetting that you are the power
    that makes and saves and sustains us.
Even when we claim your power,
  we often do so for our own success and comfort,
  ignoring your command to use your power
    on behalf of the weak, the small,
      and the vulnerable.
In Jesus Christ,
  you show us that you are on the side of all people,
    but never at the expense of the weakest among us.
Forgive us when we try to hoard you for ourselves
  and try to control who has access to your love.
Forgive us when our greed, our control,
  and our scandals keep others from knowing you.
Redeem us and transform us, O God.
Open our hearts, our lives, and our ministries,
  that we may become a doorway to your realm.

Words of Assurance (Esther 7 & 9, James 5)
God turns our sorrow into gladness
  and our times of mourning into celebration.
God hears the prayer of faith.
Be confident as we pray for one another,
  for God heals us and forgives us.

Passing the Peace of Christ (Esther 7 & 9, Psalm 124, Mark 9)
When we are rescued from danger and trouble, we know
the peace of Jesus Christ. When we are welcomed into the
reign of God, we know the peace of Jesus Christ. As those
who are rescued and welcomed, let us greet one another
with signs of the peace of Christ.

Response to the Word (Psalm 124, Mark 9)
God, make the words we have heard
  a living word in the core of our being.

Help us put our faith in no other power
    than the power of your saving love.
Make us the agents of your love,
    blocking no one's entrance
        into the presence of your love and grace.
Through Christ,
    enable us to be at peace with one another
      and to salt the earth
        with the power of your peace. Amen.

THANKSGIVING AND COMMUNION

Invitation to the Offering (Esther 7 & 9, Psalm 124)

Jesus Christ is on our side, offering us the love of God—a love that gives us all we have, a love that makes us all we are. Jesus Christ is with us in every circumstance, suffering with us when we are in trouble, and rejoicing with us when we are glad. The generosity of Christ calls us to lives of gratitude and generosity. In Jesus Christ we are given new life. Let us celebrate this life by giving generously to the work of God's redeeming love.

Offering Prayer (Esther 7 & 9, Psalm 124, Mark 9)

Giving God, we can never match your generosity.
When we are in need,
    you are at our side,
        present to us even in our darkest moments.
You rescue us from harm.
Make us into a people
    who celebrate your goodness,
    drawing others into the celebration
      of your many blessings.
Receive our offerings,
    even if they are as small
      as a drink for someone who thirsts.
Transform them into the mystery
    of your reign here and now on earth,
in the name of Jesus, your greatest gift, amen.

SENDING FORTH

Benediction (Psalm 124, James 5, Mark 9)
God has created all things.
God has rescued us from sin and suffering.
Let us go forth, seeking to be on God's side.
Jesus Christ finds us when we wander far from God.
Let us go forth, seeking to be on God's side.
The Holy Spirit empowers us to welcome all
into the reign of God's love.
Let us go forth, seeking to be on God's side,
bringing the love of Christ everywhere we go.

CONTEMPORARY OPTIONS

Contemporary Gathering Words (Psalm 124, James 5)
Jesus is on our side!
Come and rejoice.
Are you suffering?
Come and find peace.
Are you joyful?
Come and sing.
Do you need healing?
Come and pray.
Jesus is on our side!
Come and rejoice.

Praise Sentences (Psalm 124, Mark 9)
Praise God, who created all that is.
Thanks be to God, who is on our side.
Praise God, who rescues us in times of need.
Thanks be to God, who is on our side.
Praise God, who welcomes all into God's reign.
Thanks be to God, who is on our side.

OCTOBER 7, 2012

Nineteenth Sunday after Pentecost /
World Communion Sunday

Deborah Sokolove

COLOR

Green

SCRIPTURE READINGS

Job 1:1; 2:1-10; Psalm 26 (or Psalm 25); Hebrews 1:1-4; 2:5-12; Mark 10:2-16

THEME IDEAS

Even when God allows us to be tested, we are called to give God thanks and praise. We share in the glory and inheritance of Jesus, who is not ashamed to call us brothers and sisters.

INVITATION AND GATHERING

Call to Worship (Psalm 26; Hebrews 1, 2)

In the great congregation, let us bless the Holy One.
With songs of thanksgiving,
we retell God's wondrous deeds.
We love the house in which God dwells
and the place where God's glory shines forth.
Proclaim God's name to all the world!
In the midst of the congregation,
we praise God's holy name.

Opening Prayer (Job 1, 2; Hebrews 1, 2)
  Holy Mystery, Protector of the faithful,
    glorious Spirit of wonder, Bread of heaven,
    you have made us a little lower than the angels
      and crowned us with glory and honor.
  You have called us to be your witnesses,
    to proclaim the good news
      in good times and in bad.
  Sanctify us and help us see ourselves in you,
    the living body of the risen Christ,
      broken and poured out to feed a hungry world. Amen.

PROCLAMATION AND RESPONSE

Prayer of Confession (Job 2:10, Psalm 26)
  God of steadfast love,
  we have ignored your many gifts;
  we have forgotten to give thanks in all things.
    We have taken for granted the air we breathe,
    the food that nourishes our bodies,
    even the love of family and friends.
    We have forgotten that all these gifts
    come from you.
  We have sinned with our lips and in our hearts.
  Unlike your servant Job,
  when we are tested we do not say,
  "Shall we receive the good at the hand of God,
  and not receive the bad?"
    Forgive our selfish ways,
    and turn our hearts to you.

Words of Assurance (Psalm 26; Hebrews 1, 2)
  Even before we ask, God promises to redeem us
    and forgive us.
  In God's abundant grace,
    our feet stand on level ground
    and we are clothed in honor and glory.
    Amen.

Passing the Peace of Christ

As brothers and sisters in Christ, let us give one another
signs of peace:
The peace of Christ be with you, always.
And also with you.

Response to the Word (Mark 10)

Holy Mystery, Bread of heaven, Spirit of wonder,
Protector of the innocent,
by your word you have made us
your grateful children,
open to the gift of life
in your Spirit. **Amen.**

THANKSGIVING AND COMMUNION

Offering Prayer (Psalm 26; Hebrews 1, 2)

Holy Giver of all that we need,
you have filled our hearts with joy
and our hands with overflowing abundance.
With thanks and joy, we bring these gifts,
offering ourselves in communion with you
and with all creation. Amen.

Great Thanksgiving

Christ be with you.
And also with you.
Lift up your hearts.
We lift them up to God.
Let us give our thanks to the Holy One.
It is right to give our thanks and praise.
It is a right, a good, and a joyful thing,
always and everywhere to give our thanks to you,
Ruler of the Universe,
for you bring forth grain from the earth,
and fruit from the vine.
You make the rain to fall in its season,
and the sun to shine, giving light and warmth
to all your creatures.

By your word, the trees give their fruit,
the crops and grasses flourish,
and all your creatures grow in grace.
And so, with your creatures on earth
and all the heavenly chorus,
we praise your name
and join their unending hymn, saying:
**Holy, holy, holy One, God of power and might,
heaven and earth are full of your glory.
Hosanna in the highest. Blessed is the one
who comes in your holy name.
Hosanna in the highest.**

Holy are you, and holy is your child, Jesus Christ.
When he saw the little children, he called them to him,
taking them up in his arms,
laying his hands on them, and blessing them.
In his suffering and death,
he taught us the true meaning of love,
of accepting and doing your will
for the healing of the world.

(Words of Institution)
And so, in remembrance of your mighty acts
in Jesus Christ, we proclaim the mystery of faith.
**Christ has died.
Christ has risen.
Christ will come again.**

Pour out your Holy Spirit on us gathered here,
and on these gifts of bread and wine.
Make them be for us the body and blood of Christ,
that we may become one with Christ,
one with each other, and one in communion
with you and with all the world.

Protector of the innocent, Spirit of grace,
Bread of heaven, we praise you now,
tomorrow, and always.
Amen.

SENDING FORTH

Benediction (Psalm 26; Hebrews 1, 2)
Go out in wonder and joy,
clothing everyone you meet in honor and glory.
Amen.

CONTEMPORARY OPTIONS

Contemporary Gathering Words (Psalm 26; Hebrews 1, 2)
We love the house in which God dwells,
and the place where God's glory shines forth.
Let us bless the Holy One,
going forth with songs of thanksgiving
to retell the stories of God's wondrous deeds.

Praise Sentences (Psalm 26; Hebrews 1, 2)
Proclaim God's name to all the world!
We praise God's holy name, now and forever!

OCTOBER 14, 2012

Twentieth Sunday after Pentecost
B. J. Beu

COLOR
Green

SCRIPTURE READINGS
Job 23:1-9, 16-17; Psalm 22:1-15; Hebrews 4:12-16;
Mark 10:17-31

THEME IDEAS
There are times when we feel abandoned by God. While
Psalm 139 wonders where we can go to flee from God's
presence, today's reading from Job and Psalm 22 wonder
where God can be found when calamity strikes. In the book
of Hebrews, Jesus, who quotes Psalm 22 while hanging on
the cross, sympathizes with us in our weakness. And even
in the Gospel, a man blessed with riches, a man who has
obeyed the commandments since his youth, wonders what
he must do to be saved. Not a question you ask if you feel
connected to God. While there is a time for praise, these lections remind us that there is a time for grief, a time for calling out our woes to the One who often seems so far away.

INVITATION AND GATHERING

Call to Worship (Job 23, Psalm 22, Hebrews 4)
We cry out to God,
but no one answers.

We feel forsaken and lost,
abandoned and alone.
We search for God before and behind us,
but God is not there.
We search for God above and beneath us,
but come away empty.
We look for God on our left
and on our right.
We cannot perceive the One we seek.
Our source of help is far from us.
Yet, even now we will commit ourselves to the Lord.
Even now we will put our trust in our God.
For Christ sympathizes with us in our weakness,
offering grace and mercy.
With boldness, we look to the throne of grace
in our time of need.

Opening Prayer (Job 23, Psalm 22, Hebrews 4)
Elusive One,
be near us in our need.
We are poured out like water.
Our bones are out of joint.
Our hearts are like wax,
melted within our breasts.
We lie in the dust of death.
Since our birth you have watched over us,
as a mother watches over her children
in whom she delights.
Come to us swiftly and be with us now,
for the darkness threatens to swallow us whole.
Help us in our weakness,
that we may receive your mercy and grace
in our time of need. Amen.

PROCLAMATION AND RESPONSE

Prayer of Confession (Mark 10, Stewardship)
Compassionate One,
you set before us the ways of life and death,

giving us the very keys to eternal life,
   yet we turn away.
The cost seems too high.
We would show you perfect love,
   if we didn't have to give up our riches.
We would offer you perfect devotion,
   if we didn't have to alter our selfish ways.
We would present to you our very lives,
   if we could only do so in comfort.
Left to ourselves, we are lost and alone.
Forgive our reluctance to believe
   that with you, all things are possible,
   with you, we find our way home. Amen.

Assurance of Pardon (Mark 10:26-27)

Christ's words challenge us to the core.
Who then can be saved?
With mortals, it is impossible, but not for God.
For God, all things are possible.
Thanks be to God!

Invitation to the Word (Hebrews 4:12-13)

Let us listen attentively to holy scripture, for as the author of Hebrews writes: "The word of God is living and active, sharper than any two-edged sword, piercing until it divides soul from spirit, joints from marrow; it is able to judge the thoughts and intentions of the heart. And before [God] no creature is hidden, but all are naked and laid bare to the eyes of the one to whom we must render an account." Listen attentively, and you will live.

Response to the Word (Psalm 22:4-5)

In God our ancestors trusted and were delivered. To God our ancestors cried and were saved. In God our ancestors hoped and were not put to shame. Let us take a lesson from those who went before us, that we too may have life and have it abundantly.

OCTOBER 14, 2012

THANKSGIVING AND COMMUNION

Offering Prayer (Psalm 22, Mark 10, Stewardship)
Eternal God,
even when you seem far away,
you take us safely from the womb of life
and suckle us at your breast;
even when we feel forsaken by your love,
you deliver us from evil.
Accept these gifts as tribute and thanks
for all we have received from your hand.
Transform our selfish hearts
into vessels of overflowing generosity,
that we might know the joy
of your salvation,
which is eternal life
through Jesus Christ, our Lord. Amen.

SENDING FORTH

Benediction (Psalm 22, Hebrews 4)
Even when we feel poured out like water,
Christ offers us grace and mercy.
Even when God seems far away,
Christ gives us hope and encouragement.
Even when we feel abandoned and alone,
Christ brings us peace and contentment.
Christ is with us always.
Thanks be to God!

CONTEMPORARY OPTIONS

Contemporary Gathering Words (Psalm 22, Hebrews 4, Mark 10)
We're lost and can't find our way.
**Come before the throne of grace
and find mercy.**

We're poured out like water,
our hearts are like melted wax.
> **Come before the throne of grace**
> **and find mercy.**
Is there anything we can do to find eternal life?
> **Come before the throne of grace**
> **and find mercy.**
For God, all things are possible.
> **Come before the throne of grace**
> **and find mercy.**

Praise Sentences (Psalm 22, Hebrews 4)

Holy is our God and greatly to be praised.
> **Holy is our God and greatly to be praised.**
Glory to Christ and to the throne of grace.
> **Glory to Christ and to the throne of grace.**
Holy is our God and greatly to be praised.
> **Holy is our God and greatly to be praised.**

OCTOBER 21, 2012

Twenty-first Sunday after Pentecost
B. J. Beu

COLOR
Green

SCRIPTURE READINGS
Job 38:1-7, (34-41); Psalm 104:1-9, 24, 35c; Hebrews 5:1-10;
Mark 10:35-45

THEME IDEAS
Great is God's power. God stretches the heavens like a
tent, sets the earth on firm foundations, and covers the
waters of the deep. We long for a taste of this power, unless we get caught in the whirlwind like Job. We long to
possess this power, but Christ reminds us that true power
is found in service. To embrace Christ's glory and sit at
his right hand is to hang with thieves, to dine with sinners, to serve tirelessly. Job was a faithful follower of his
God, yet was not spared calamity. Christ's disciples are
invited to drink the cup that Jesus drank and to be baptized into his suffering and death. And we wonder why
more people do not flock to churches that truly preach the
gospel! Yet this is our road and the nature of true power.
And when we follow in Christ's steps, serve with generosity, live with kindness, walk with humility, care with
compassion, and serve in Christ's name, God draws us to

Christ's side and clothes us with the greatest power and glory of all—the power and glory of love.

INVITATION AND GATHERING

Call to Worship (Job 38, Psalm 104)
Behold God in the heavens,
stretched out like a tent.
Hear God's voice in the winds,
whispering words of life and love.
Witness God's glory in fire and flame,
dancing colors of orange and red.
Take refuge in God on the mountains,
silent, strong, and immovable.
Rest in the wisdom of God,
hidden in the clouds above and seas below.
Bless the Lord, O my soul,
and bless God's holy name.

Opening Prayer (Job 38, Psalm 104, Mark 10)
God of majesty and might,
may your untamable wisdom
blow through our lives
like a mighty whirlwind,
upsetting our self-serving truths
and preoccupied ways.
Disrupt our sunny assurance of your favor
with a thunderous call to serve our neighbor.
Stir up a tempest within our hearts,
that we may behold the glory of your baptism—
a baptism into kindness and compassion,
love and generosity of spirit.
Clothe us with your love,
that we may be a people of hope,
a people of prayer,
a people of true spirit,
through Christ, our Lord. Amen.

PROCLAMATION AND RESPONSE

Prayer of Confession (Job 38, Mark 10)
We are so sure of ourselves, O God.
In the midst of our suffering,
    we wonder how it could happen to us;
    we wonder why you allowed it to happen at all.
How easily we forget
    that Job was blameless in your sight,
        yet found himself in the path of the tornado.
How quickly we look for answers
    to questions beyond our ability to comprehend.
How often we darken counsel
    with words of accusation without wisdom.
Forgive us, Lord.
Forgive us when we seek to sit at your right hand,
    rather than accepting the role of the servant.
Forgive us when we look for comfort and ease
    in your cup and in your baptism.
Answer us in your whirlwind once more.
Teach us that suffering is not sent to punish,
    but that through our suffering,
        we may better understand and heal
            the pain of others. Amen.

Words of Assurance (Hebrews 5)
Christ, our High Priest, was made perfect
    through the fire of his suffering and death.
Christ, our High Priest, was made perfect
    through a love so strong
    that he refused to take the easy path,
    the safe path,
    the path of earthly power and glory.
In Jesus Christ, who intercedes on our behalf,
    we are forgiven and offered salvation in his name.

Passing the Peace of Christ (Hebrews 5)
In the name of Christ, the begotten Child of God, let us
turn to one another with joy and share signs of the un-
conditional love of God.

Response to the Word (Job 38, Psalm 104)
Almighty God,
> you put wisdom in our inward parts;
> you grant understanding to our minds;
> you make the winds your messengers
> > and the clouds your ministers.

Give us the wisdom to discern your word
> in every detail of our lives.

And give us the strength to drink from your cup
> and to be baptized with your baptism,
> > that we may know that true strength and power
> > > comes from a life of service to others
> > > > in your holy name. Amen.

THANKSGIVING AND COMMUNION

Offering Prayer (Psalm 104, Mark 10)
Creator God, you bring rain to the earth
> and food to your creatures.

We thank you for the abundance of our lives
> and praise you for the opportunity to share
> > what you have so freely given.

As we present these gifts,
> we dedicate our lives to your service,
> > that all may know the blessing of your bounty. Amen.

SENDING FORTH

Benediction (Mark 10)
Bless us with your power, O God,
> **the power to serve and make a difference
> in our world.**

Bless us with your love, beloved Son,
> **the love that heals all wounds
> and brings comfort to the afflicted.**

Bless us with your glory, Great Spirit,
> **the glory of lives filled with purpose,
> the glory of lives touched by grace.**

Go forth to serve and to love.
Go forth as beloved children of God!

CONTEMPORARY OPTIONS

Contemporary Gathering Words or Call to Worship (Job 38, Psalm 104, Mark 10)

God speaks from the whirlwind:
"Seek me,
like a lion pursues its prey."
God hearkens from the clouds:
"Thirst for me,
like the parched ground thirsts for rain."
God calls from the heavens:
"Sing to me,
like the morning star sang at creation."
God beckons from the waters:
"Cling to me,
like a drowning sailor clings to a lifeline."
God calls to us now.
We are here, Lord.
Lead us to life.

Praise Sentences (Psalm 104, Mark 10)

Bless the Lord my soul,
and bless God's holy name.
Majesty and praise to the One
who teaches us to serve.
Majesty and praise to the One who gives us life!
Bless the Lord my soul,
and bless God's holy name.

OCTOBER 28, 2012

Reformation Sunday

Jamie D. Greening

COLOR
Green

SCRIPTURE READINGS
Job 42:1-6, 10-17; Psalm 34:1-8 (19-22); Hebrews 7:23-28; Mark 10:46-52

THEME IDEAS
At first glance these lections seem to have very little in common. Yet each carries an undercurrent of putting things right. As such, these readings pair perfectly with the Reformation theme of this day—that which was not right has been put right! The driving narrative is that of blind Bartimaeus: our desire for Christ is an act of faith that God uses to bring restoration. Jesus restores, but Bartimaeus's desire and belief are necessary to make the restoration possible.

INVITATION AND GATHERING

Call to Worship (Psalm 34)
Bless the Lord at all times.
Let everyone bless God.
Praise the Lord continually.
Let everyone praise Christ.

Our souls boast in the Lord.
We boast in the Spirit's greatness.
With one voice, we magnify and exalt the Lord,
for God has delivered us and made us whole.
Exalt our God, the Lord of life.

Opening Prayer (Hebrews 7, Mark 10)
Great Triune God,
through Jesus Christ,
our great and eternal High Priest,
we give you praise
and consecrate ourselves to follow you.
As we worship you
and celebrate your glorious resurrection,
open our eyes so that we may see—
open the eyes of our mind
to learning and understanding;
open the eyes of our heart,
to love and compassion;
open the eyes of our soul,
to see our spiritual selves
during our time of worship. Amen.

PROCLAMATION AND RESPONSE

Prayer of Confession (Job 42, Psalm 34, Hebrews 7, Mark 10)
Mystical, transcendent God,
there is so much of life
we simply do not know.
In our arrogance,
we utter what we do not understand.
Rescue us, O Lord, from our afflictions.
Restore us, O God, from our self-inflicted wounds.
Have mercy on us, Son of David, Son of God,
and save us by your unending intercession.

Words of Assurance (Psalm 34, Hebrews 7, Mark 10)
Cry out to Christ, our great High Priest,
for he has saved us.

Our faith has made us well, brought us forgiveness,
and granted us peace.

Passing the Peace of Christ (Job 42)

That we may come through life's ups and downs, live to
a good and full age, and see God's mercy to our children
and children's children, let us bless one another with these
words of peace: "May you live to see God's mercy to four
generations."

Response to the Word (Mark 10)

Like Jesus leaving Jericho,
your word has passed before us today.
Have mercy on us, Lord!
Others have told us to be quiet.
Many have tried to lure us away, yet we desire you.
Have mercy on us, Lord!
Then you spoke to us and called us by name,
filling us with your word.
Have mercy on us, Lord!
You ask us what we want, what we need.
There are so many things we hold in our heart:
home, family, health, our nation—
but you know our greatest need.
Lord, let us see as you see.
Have mercy on us, Lord! Amen.

THANKSGIVING AND COMMUNION

Offering Prayer (Psalm 34, Job 42)

You invite us, God,
to taste and see that you are good.
Well, we have tasted
and you are truly good.
As a token of our gratitude
and a reflection of our devotion,
we give back to you from our abundance.
Multiply the gifts of our hands,
that they may double what we could do alone.
To the glory and service of Jesus, amen.

Prayer of Thanksgiving

We give you thanks this day
for the mighty and subtle ways
you work in the lives of your people.
You are a God who restores.
You restored Job from his misery.
You restored David from his afflictions.
You restored the true meaning of priesthood.
You restored Bartimaeus's sight.
You restored the church to proper doctrine
at Nicaea.
You restored justification by faith
using Wittenberg's door.
You restored the preaching of the gospel
through Wesley.
You restore families that are broken.
You restore ministries in peril.
You restore our souls with your Holy Spirit.
You restore the shattered hearts
that have forgotten how much
you love them.
Almighty Father, Son, and Holy Spirit,
we thank you for what you have done,
are doing, and will do. Amen.

SENDING FORTH

Benediction (Mark 10)

Go! Your faith has made you well.
**We go, knowing that our faith
has been made stronger.**
Go! Follow him on the way.
We go, knowing Jesus is the way.

CONTEMPORARY OPTIONS

Contemporary Gathering Words (Mark 10)

Take heart, Christ is calling us.
He beckons us to come . . .

Come near to him.
Stand before Christ.
"What do you want me to do?" he asks.
We have come here;
Were drawn here.
We desire to be here.
To have our sight restored.

Praise Sentences (Psalm 34)

Worship the Lord.
Hallelujah!
Look to the Lord.
We are not ashamed.
Hallelujah!

NOVEMBER 1, 2012

All Saints Day
Deborah Sokolove

COLOR
White

SCRIPTURE READINGS
Isaiah 25:6-9; Psalm 24; Revelation 21:1-6a; John 11:32-44

THEME IDEAS
The true home of God is among humans. In the realm of God, all that is broken will be healed, and all will live in peace, joy, and eternal life.

INVITATION AND GATHERING

Call to Worship (Isaiah 25, Psalm 24)
The earth and all that is in it belongs to the Holy One.
   Look, here is our God,
   for whom we have waited.
This is the Holy One, for whom we have waited.
   Let us be glad and rejoice in our salvation.
Who shall ascend the hill of the Holy One?
And who shall stand in this holy place?
   We come, seeking the face of God.

Opening Prayer (Psalm 24, Revelation 21)
Faithful Redeemer,
   you are the beginning and ending of all things.

You promise to wipe away every tear,
  that death and mourning will be no more.
You make your home among us,
  and abide with us as our God.
Teach us to live as the saints you call us to be,
    that we may truly be your people,
    living and doing your will,
        in the name of Jesus, who is the Christ. Amen.

PROCLAMATION AND RESPONSE

Prayer of Confession (Psalm 24, Revelation 21, John 11)
Patient, Forgiving Spirit, we come seeking your face.
  We hold on to ancient angers and hurts,
  and refuse to believe that you alone
  can make all things new.
Like Mary and Martha,
we have forgotten your promises of eternal life.
  Like the crowd that mourned for Lazarus,
  we have not believed that we would see
  your glory.
Forgive our unbelief, O God.
  Bring us back, and restore our trust in you.

Words of Assurance (Revelation 21)
The Holy One shows us a vision
  of a new heaven and a new earth,
    where everyone will live in peace and blessing.
Trusting in God's promise to wipe away all our tears,
  in the name of Christ, you are forgiven.
  In the name of Christ, you are forgiven.
  Glory to God. Amen.

Passing the Peace of Christ
Rejoicing in the love of the one for whom we wait, let us
exchange signs of Christ's peace:
May the peace of Christ be with you,
today and always.
  May the peace of Christ be with you,
  today and always.

Response to the Word (Revelation 21, John 11)
Alpha and Omega, beginning and ending of all creation,
in your word we are unbound from death, and brought
out into eternal life in you.
Amen.

THANKSGIVING AND COMMUNION

Offering Prayer (Isaiah 25, Revelation 21)
Generous Giver of all that we need,
accept these gifts of simple bread
and ordinary wine,
that we may one day share in your holy feast
spread out through all the world.
We pray in the name of Jesus, your holy child,
who sets the table for all people—
a table of rich food and abundant joy.
Amen.

Great Thanksgiving
Christ be with you.
And also with you.
Lift up your hearts.
We lift them up to God.
Let us give our thanks to the Holy One.
It is right to give our thanks and praise.
It is a right, a good, and a joyful thing
always and everywhere to give our thanks to you,
Alpha and Omega, beginning and ending
of all creation.
In the days of Isaiah, you promised to lead
all the nations to your holy mountain,
and swallow up death forever.
You have revealed the coming of a new heaven
and new earth, in which every tear
will be wiped from our eyes,
and all will feast at your heavenly banquet.

And so, with your saints now on earth
    and all the company of heaven,
    we praise your name
    and join their unending hymn, saying:
    Holy, holy, holy One, God of power and might,
        heaven and earth are full of your glory.
    Hosanna in the highest. Blessed is the one
        who comes in your holy name.
    Hosanna in the highest.
Holy are you, and holy is your child, Jesus Christ.
When he raised Lazarus from the grave,
    he showed us all your glory,
    giving thanks only to you and praising your name.
(Words of Institution and Memorial Acclamation)

Pour out your Holy Spirit on us gathered here,
    and on these gifts of bread and wine.
Make them be for us the body and blood of Christ,
    so that we may become one with Christ,
    one with each other, and one in ministry
    to all the world, until all things are made new.
Alpha and Omega, Beginning and Ending,
    Spirit of new beginnings,
    we praise your holy, eternal, triune name. **Amen.**

SENDING FORTH

Benediction (Psalm 24, Revelation 21)
Go into the world as the living body of Christ,
bringing eternal life to all who seek God's face.
    Amen.

CONTEMPORARY OPTIONS

Contemporary Gathering Words (Psalm 24)
The earth and all that is in it belongs to the Holy One.
    Look, this is our God,
    for whom we have waited.

Will you come to the hill of the Holy One?
We come, seeking the face of God.
Come, let us worship.

Praise Sentences (Psalm 24)
This is the Holy One for whom we have waited.
We rejoice in our salvation.
This is the Holy One for whom we have waited.
We rejoice in our salvation.

NOVEMBER 4, 2012

Twenty-third Sunday after Pentecost
Mary J. Scifres

COLOR
Green

SCRIPTURE READINGS
Ruth 1:1-18; Psalm 146; Hebrews 9:11-14; Mark 12:28-34

THEME IDEAS
Love. Love God, love self, love neighbor. The gospel in a word is love! Jesus and the scribe agree in today's Gospel lesson: the central tenet of faith is love. The foreigner Ruth, recently widowed, knows this instinctively when she follows her loving heart and travels with her mother-in-law to a land she has never known. This love connection may be taken lightly on reality television, but not so in our scriptures. The call to love demands courage and strength, sacrifice and servanthood. The call to love is God's call to all who would follow Christ.

INVITATION AND GATHERING

Call to Worship (Ruth 1, Mark 12)
Come into the land of God.
We come seeking the land of love.
Live as the people of Christ.
We gather to grow as a community of love.

Follow in the ways of the Lord.
We move forward on the path of love.
Come, young and old, friend and foreigner,
for all are welcome here.
We come to live and grow in the love of Christ.
Praise God for this wonderful gift!

—OR—

Call to Worship or Praise Sentences (Psalm 146)
Praise the God of love!
We rejoice in this abundant love!
Praise the God of hope!
We sing praise for this life-giving hope!
Praise the God of new beginnings!
We give thanks for this chance for new life.

Opening Prayer (Ruth 1, Mark 12)
O God,
you are our God
and we come as your people on earth.
Gather us in,
that we may remember the ties
that bind us together in your love.
Write your law upon our hearts,
that others may find us to be
generous and loving friends.
Strengthen us by your Spirit,
that we may live in love—
a love that transforms our lives
even as we help to transform
the lives of others.
In the hope of your miraculous love, we pray. Amen.

PROCLAMATION AND RESPONSE

Prayer of Confession (Ruth 1, Psalm 146, Mark 12)
Helper God,
be the hope that overcomes our despair;

be the love that overcomes our hatred;
be the mercy that overcomes our sin.
Set us free from the prisons of our own making,
and release us from the bonds that bind us.
Forgive us and watch over us.
Welcome us home
into the loving arms of your mercy.
In Christ's name, we pray. Amen.

Words of Assurance (Mark 12)

You are not far from the kingdom of God,
for in Christ we are given grace and forgiveness.
Praise God for this marvelous gift!

Passing the Peace of Christ (Ruth 1, Mark 12)

As the church, we gather together in the spirit of Ruth and
Naomi. Where you go, I will go. Where you dwell, I will
dwell. Your God will be my God, and your people will be
my people. We are bound as one body in love of God,
neighbor, and self. Let us share this message of unity as
we exchange signs of peace and love.

Response to the Word (Mark 12)

Love God with all your heart
and mind and soul and strength.
We love as God loves us!
Love your neighbors as yourself,
with kindness and care.
We love as God loves us!
Love yourself with gentleness,
with mercy and grace.
We love as God loves us!

THANKSGIVING AND COMMUNION

Invitation to the Offering (Psalm 146)

As the people of God, we are called to be justice for the
oppressed, food for the hungry, freedom for the impris-
oned, and sight for the blind. Let us lift up those in need
as we share gifts for the church's mission.

Offering Prayer (Psalm 146, Mark 12)
  God of justice and love,
    transform these offerings,
      that they may be gifts of justice and love
        for a world in need of hope and help.
  Let love flow through these offerings,
    that they may become gifts of love for the world.

SENDING FORTH

Benediction (Ruth 1, Mark 12)
  Go to love God and neighbor.
    We go forth in the love of God!
  Go to welcome the stranger.
    We go forth with love for the world!

CONTEMPORARY OPTIONS

Contemporary Gathering Words (Ruth 1, Mark 12)
  Here in this place, there are no foreigners,
    for all are welcome in God's house.
  Here in this worship, there is only acceptance,
    for love is the language of faith.
  Here in our lives, there are no divisions,
    for God dwells in each of us.
  Come, let us worship in unity and love.

Praise Sentences (Psalm 146, Mark 12)
  I will praise Christ as long as I live!
  Praise God for the wonders of love!
  I will praise Christ as long as I live!
  Praise God for the wonders of love!

NOVEMBER 11, 2012

Twenty-fourth Sunday after Pentecost
B. J. Beu

COLOR
Green

SCRIPTURE READINGS
Ruth 3:1-5; 4:13-17; Psalm 127 (or Psalm 42);
Hebrews 9:24-28; Mark 12:38-44

THEME IDEAS
Psalm 127 says it all: "Unless the LORD builds the house,
those who build it labor in vain" (v. 1). Naomi thinks she
is building a house for herself and for Ruth, but God is
building a house for the whole people of Israel. The
psalmist reminds us that children are a heritage from
God—but a heritage, as Naomi finds out, that can disap-
pear at any moment. Hebrews reminds us that our hopes
are founded upon Christ, and not upon any sanctuary
built with human hands. Finally, while the Temple system
relies upon human generosity to keep things running,
God views the humble offering of a poor widow to be of
infinitely greater value. As the Pharisees show, human
scheming and posturing go only so far. If God doesn't
build the house, it is doomed to come crashing down
around us.

INVITATION AND GATHERING

Call to Worship (Psalm 127:1)
Unless the Lord builds the house,
the builders labor in vain.
Build us into a spiritual house, O God,
that we may truly be your people.
Unless the Lord guards the city,
the guards keep watch in vain.
Guard our hearts and minds, O God,
that we may walk in your ways.
Unless the Lord is the center of worship,
our words and praise are in vain.
Be with us now, O God,
that we may taste eternity.

Opening Prayer (Ruth 3–4, Psalm 127, Hebrews 9, Mark 12)
God of infinite possibility,
the world says no,
but you say yes;
the world warns against marrying foreigners
but you transform our boldness
into a blessing for all people;
the world values the benevolence of the rich
but you cherish the sacrifice of the poor.
Build us into a house with a firm foundation,
that the labors of our hands
may endure the sands of time
and the ravages of age.
Guard the walls of our spirit,
that we may withstand the temptation
to put our faith in things that do not endure
rather than in the sanctuary of your love. Amen.

PROCLAMATION AND RESPONSE

Prayer of Confession (Mark 12)
Holy Seer,
you see us as we really are,

as we can be,
as we are created to be;
you see us with loving eyes.
But we cannot see as you see.
We lack your vision,
your capacity to love.
We cannot seem to love ourselves,
so we cannot truly love others.
We puff ourselves up,
seeking the praise of others,
relishing ridicule for those we feel are beneath us.
Forgive us, O God.
Help us love ourselves,
that we may truly love others.
Help us give freely of ourselves,
that we may appreciate the gifts of others,
even when they seem small by comparison.
In Christ's name, we pray. Amen.

Assurance of Pardon (Hebrews 9)

Christ entered into heaven itself
to appear before God on our behalf.
Rejoice in the knowledge that in Christ
our sins are forgiven.

Response to the Word (Ruth 3–4)

Naomi had no idea that by securing a husband for Ruth,
she was securing the future of the whole people of Israel.
So it often is when we follow the impulse of our hearts.
Do more than hear the word of God—live it. Live it with
love, and do not be surprised if you find yourself building
the realm of God.

THANKSGIVING AND COMMUNION

Invitation to the Offering or Prayer of Confession (Mark 12, Stewardship)

Multiplier of grace,
we love the story of the poor widow

who is praised by Jesus
for offering her small gift.
We tell ourselves that you prefer a meager gift
over large sums given by the rich.
We justify our token contributions,
convincing ourselves that we too are poor,
forgetting that in your eyes,
we are the world's rich,
ignoring the inconvenient truth
that unlike the poor widow
we never give all we have.
Forgive us when we justify our selfish ways.
Grant us generous hearts,
that we may be opened to the joy of helping others,
that we may know the satisfaction
of helping to heal the world.

Offering Prayer (Ruth 3–4, Mark 12)
Multiply our gifts, holy One,
that all your people may be built
into a spiritual house—
a house that no earthly calamity
can bring down.
Free our hearts, gracious God,
that like Naomi and Ruth before us,
your great purposes
may work through our love. Amen.

SENDING FORTH

Benediction (Psalm 127, Hebrews 9)
God builds us into a spiritual house.
Christ offers us fullness of life
in God's kingdom, which has no end.
God guards the fortress of our spirit.
Christ offers us fullness of life
in God's kingdom, which has no end.
God opens our hearts to heal the world.

Christ offers us fullness of life
in God's kingdom, which has no end.
Go with God.

CONTEMPORARY OPTIONS

Contemporary Gathering Words (Psalm 127)
How do we build something that will last?
**Unless the Lord builds the house,
the builders labor in vain.**
How do we stay safe?
**Unless the Lord guards the city,
the guards keep watch in vain.**
How do we worship in spirit and truth?
**Unless the Lord is the center of worship,
our words and praise are in vain.**

Praise Sentences (Ruth 3–4, Mark 12)
Praise the One who restores our fortunes.
Praise the One who rebuilds our lives.
Praise the One who lifts up the widow.
Praise the One who brings down the proud.
Praise God.
Praise God.
Praise God.

NOVEMBER 18, 2012

Twenty-fifth Sunday after Pentecost
Sara Dunning Lambert

COLOR

Green

SCRIPTURE READINGS

1 Samuel 1:4-20; 1 Samuel 2:1-10 (or Psalm 113);
Hebrews 10:11-14 (15-18), 19-25; Mark 13:1-8

THEME IDEAS

As she copes with the tragedy of childlessness, Hannah, the mother of sorrows, praises God continually. After the birth of Samuel, Hannah, the mother of joy, still exults in her Lord. Her faith is a source of comfort, strength, and guidance throughout her life. The imagery of the lowly lifted up and the proud brought down by God's knowledge and authority brings truth as well as warning. Psalm 113 echoes Hannah's exaltation, blessing and glorifying the Lord who is to be praised. The New Testament readings add the dimension that Christ has shown us the "new and living way" of faith, hope, and love. As we travel together as disciples in Christ, striving to love God and one another, we must encourage and support our individual and corporate journeys. While there will be many challenges, both known and unknown, our strength and comfort are always in the Lord.

INVITATION AND GATHERING

Call to Worship (1 Samuel 1, Psalm 113, Hebrews 10, Mark 13)

My strength is exalted in my God.
Despite sorrows and sadness, anxieties and vexations,
we praise your name, O Lord.
   For the power of the Lord gives me strength,
   and the love of the Lord gives me hope.
With Hannah, the mother of sorrows,
we bless the name of the Lord, today and forever.
From the rising of the sun to its setting, God is with us.
   Blessed be the name of the Lord.
   We praise your holy name, O God.
From Hannah, the mother of joy,
we learn the bounty of unwavering hope.
   Let your servant find favor in your sight,
   O Lord.
Hardship is a constant companion.
We must rely on the selfless example of Christ
to show us the way to truth, life, and love. **Amen.**

—OR—

Call to Worship (1 Samuel 1 & 2)

Come worship the Lord who is in our midst today.
   There is no Holy One like our God.
Like Hannah of old, we raise our voices
to praise the Lord of strength.
   There is no Rock like our God.
We prepare to listen and learn
with open hearts and open minds.
   There is no Source of knowledge like our God.
We trust that righteousness will come
on the heels of God's judgment.
   There is no Justice like our God.
May the Son of our God lead us into faith.
   There is no Guide like our God.
Come worship the Lord who is in our midst today.

Opening Prayer (1 Samuel 1, Hebrews 10)
Holy One,
  there is no God like you.
In praise and thanksgiving,
  we come before you
    ready to learn of your power,
    ready to follow your path for our lives.
Through days of jubilation as well as dejection,
  help us realize your influence in the world.
We ask simply for ears to hear,
  eyes to see,
    and minds to comprehend
      the blessings you bestow. Amen.

PROCLAMATION AND RESPONSE

Prayer of Confession (1 Samuel 1, Hebrews 10, Mark 13)
Rock of Salvation,
  you give children to the barren
    and strength to the feeble;
  you exalt the poor
    and lift up the needy.
We praise your holy name from morning to night,
  yet we build walls that separate us:
    from you, from one another, from the world,
      even from ourselves.
We place stumbling blocks
  in the way of goodness and truth.
We are led astray by promises of earthly treasure.
We confess our fallibility
  and seek solace in the mother of our joy.
Teach us to pray and praise without pause,
  confessing hope ceaselessly.
Guide us in our efforts
  to encourage one another,
  to work together for good in the world,
  and to prepare for the day of the Lord.

Words of Assurance (Hebrews 10)
Our hearts are sprinkled clean and our bodies washed
with the water of God's love.
Through the gift of Jesus Christ,
God assures us that we are pardoned, forgiven,
absolved, and released from our sin.

Passing the Peace of Christ (Hebrews 10)
Christ offers peace to all who will accept it. Share the love
of God and encourage one another with hope as you greet
one another in faith:
The peace of Christ be with you.
And also with you! Amen.

Response to the Word (1 Samuel 1, Hebrews 10)
Like God's servant of old, we glorify the Rock of our faith.
As a mother delights in her children, so our God delights
when we follow the way of Christ. May these words live
in our hearts and turn our minds toward the one who
brings us life.

THANKSGIVING AND COMMUNION

Offering Prayer (1 Samuel 1, Psalm 113, Hebrews 10, Mark 13)
Today, O Lord,
we offer you our sacrifice
of time, energy, and love,
knowing full well they are mere tokens
of the awesome faith you inspire within us.
Accept these gifts,
that they may continue the good work in Christ—
in our church, in our community,
and in the world.
Blessed be the name of the Lord!

Invitation to Communion (1 Samuel 1, Hebrews 10, Mark 13)

There is no Holy One like the Lord, no Rock like our God. From sorrow to joy, we celebrate and exalt our God together. Our Loving Parent, who entreats us to love one another, has offered us the beloved Son, the Christ. Our lives are redeemed with this amazing sacrifice. All who embrace this gift are invited to the communion table, to share with brothers and sisters who love, encourage, and nourish one another in faith. Come, eat, drink, live.

SENDING FORTH

Benediction (1 Samuel 1, Psalm 113, Mark 13)

May the Holy One, the Rock of our salvation,
    the Mother of Sorrow and Joy,
    the Parent of the risen Christ,
    bless us now!
Join together in faith to work for truth and honesty.
As God loves you, carry that love out into the world
    in peace, hope, and faith.

—OR—

Benediction (1 Samuel 1 & 2)

Go in peace, remembering a mother's faith in God—
    a faith that provided her with comfort and strength
    in her time of need.
May you pray unfailingly, grow steadily,
    and love constantly. Amen.

CONTEMPORARY OPTIONS

Contemporary Gathering Words (1 Samuel 1, Mark 13)

We gather in the name of the Holy One, Rock of Life,
Ever Loving God, Strength and Power,
    Love and Gentleness.
Come into the fold.
Join the journey,
    and follow the way of Christ today!

—OR—

Contemporary Gathering Words (1 Samuel 1)
There is no God like our God!
   Praise God's name forever!
Come, listen to what God has in store.
   Praise God's name forever!
Sing with joy, like a mother with a newborn baby.
   Praise God's name forever!
Pray without pausing, like a father waiting for news
of a loved one.
   Praise God's name forever!
Bless God from sunup to sundown.
   Praise God's name forever!
Bless the name of the Lord forever!
   Praise God's name forever!

Praise Sentences (1 Samuel 1, Psalm 113, Hebrews 10, Mark 13)
Bless the name of the Lord forever!
The Rock of Life, the Holy One is here.
Praise God's name!
Despite misery and heartache,
   God is with us.
In times of joy and happiness,
   God is with us.
Praise God's name!
Praise God's name!
Praise God's name!

NOVEMBER 22, 2012

Thanksgiving Day

Sandra Miller

COLOR

Red or White

SCRIPTURE READINGS

Joel 2:21-27; Psalm 126; 1 Timothy 2:1-7; Matthew 6:25-33

THEME IDEAS

Reasons for abundant thanksgiving begin in the passage from Joel and continue through the passage from Matthew. With the promise of salvation for all who seek the kingdom, God has turned our tears to shouts of joy.

INVITATION AND GATHERING

Call to Worship (Joel 2, Psalm 126, Matthew 6)
God of vindication and salvation,
you alone free us from fear and worry.
You fill our mouths with laughter
and our tongues shout with joy.
Life in your love is greater than any feast.
Praise God, who has dealt wondrously with us.
The Holy One has done great things for us.
Thanks be to God.

—OR—

Call to Worship (Joel 2, Psalm 126)

Be glad and rejoice!
We rejoice in God's gifts!
Sing praises of joy!
Our mouths are filled with laughter.
With gratitude, we come.
God has done great things for us.
Shout with laughter, in sunshine and rain.
Praise God for our lives, for harvest and food.
(*Mary J. Scifres*)

Opening Prayer (Joel 2, 1 Timothy 2, Matthew 6)

Generous, Loving God,
you bring all creation into being—
the soil and rain, the bountiful harvest,
the glory of the lilies of the field.
You bless our lives with Christ Jesus,
promising that we shall eat in plenty
at his table and be satisfied.
We offer to you our prayers of thanksgiving
for the great fortune you set before us.
Merciful One,
may every living thing be strengthened
and be brought into your kingdom,
in peace and dignity. Amen.

PROCLAMATION AND RESPONSE

Prayer of Confession (Joel 2, 1 Timothy 2, Matthew 6)

Gracious God, we come to you lost in our anguish.
We are beset by fears and worry,
concerned with the things of this world.
Our faith wavers when our leaders love war
more than they value peace. Our courage fails
when we wonder whether we are worthy of salvation.
We cling to the wisdom of this world,
rather than your truth and righteousness.

Merciful God, we ask for your forgiveness.
Restore our faith and forgive our unbelief.

Words of Assurance (Joel 2, 1 Timothy 2)

God has given the early rain for your vindication.
You are forgiven and shall not be put to shame.
You are forgiven in Christ Jesus
who gave himself in ransom for us all.

Passing the Peace of Christ

Rejoice in Christ Jesus, your mediator and savior and
share signs of peace with one another:
Christ's peace be with you with thanksgiving.
Christ's peace be with you with thanksgiving.

Response to the Word (Psalm 126, 1 Timothy 2)

Holy One, you restore us and turn our tears
into shouts of joy. We receive your word
in faith and truth.
Amen.

THANKSGIVING AND COMMUNION

Offering Prayer

Bountiful God,
we look forward to your harvest each year.
Our tables overflow
with the goodness of your green earth,
but our tables pale in comparison
to the splendor that awaits us,
and all of your children,
at your heavenly banquet.
Receive these offerings,
as we thank you for your many blessings.
Help us be mindful of those who go without
as we feast and make merry
during this festive season. Amen.
(B. J. Beu)

Communion Prayer (1 Timothy 2, Matthew 6)

Holy One,
> from the bounty of your vines and fields,
>> we are transformed by the gift
>>> of your bread and cup.

You invite everyone to the table,
> filling those who are hungry
>> with food enough to eat their fill.

Let us eat and drink deeply
> with thanksgiving in our hearts,
>> in the name of Jesus, the Christ. Amen.

SENDING FORTH

Benediction (Psalm 126, 1 Timothy 2)

Greet the world with joy in your hearts.
Let peace and dignity lead your every step,
knowing that God abides with you always.
Amen.

CONTEMPORARY OPTIONS

Contemporary Gathering Words (Joel 2, 1 Timothy 2)

We come to God with gladness and rejoicing.
**We come with thanksgiving and praise
for the Holy One.**
We come with prayers for the peace of the world
to the Holy One.
**We bring our prayers to the One
who desires that everyone be saved.**

Praise Sentences (Joel 2, Psalm 126, Matthew 6)

Praise God, who takes away our fear and worry!
Praise God, who provides for our needs!
Praise God, who brings wonder and glory to our lives!
Praise God, who lives with us and restores us!

NOVEMBER 25, 2012

Christ the King / Reign of Christ Sunday
Hans Holznagel

COLOR
White

SCRIPTURE READINGS
2 Samuel 23:1-7; Psalm 132:1-12; Revelation 1:4b-8;
John 18:33-37

THEME IDEAS
Truth is spoken to power in today's Gospel, offering stark,
this-worldly contrast to the cosmic, royal imagery of the
other readings—a commentary in itself on what is valued
in Christ's reign. We are told that Jesus is the ruler of the
kings of the earth (Revelation 1:5), an enthroned descen-
dant of King David (Psalm 132:11-12), the anointed of God
(2 Samuel 23:1). But in John's passion story, he is far from
lifted up and glorified. A prisoner, he nonetheless goes
toe-to-toe with Pilate, a colonial bureaucrat of the Roman
Empire, and refuses to be trapped into calling himself
king: "You say that I am a king.... I came into the world,
to testify to the truth" (John 18:37). May truth reign.

INVITATION AND GATHERING

Call to Worship (Psalm 132:14-16)
"This is my resting place," says our God,
"for I have desired it.

"I will ... bless its provisions;
"I will satisfy its poor with bread.
"Its priests I will clothe with salvation,
"and its faithful will shout for joy."
Come then, with joy, and let us worship God.

—OR—

Call to Worship (2 Samuel 23, John 18)
Christ came to be our king.
We have come to be Christ's people.
The King of kings calls us to follow God.
We have come to be Christ's people.
Christ came to be our king.
We have come to be Christ's people.
(B. J. Beu)

Opening Prayer (Revelation 1)
With thankful hearts we pause this day
to be reminded of our grandest hope:
that the calamities, the demands,
even the blessings of this world
do not have the last word.
You are the one who was and is,
and who is yet to come—
a ruler of a different kind.
Open our hearts to the comfort, the challenge
and the mystery of this good news.
In the name of Jesus Christ, your faithful witness,
we pray. Amen.

PROCLAMATION AND RESPONSE

Prayer of Confession (Revelation 1, John 18, 2 Samuel 23)
God of all creation,
before time and beyond space,
we admit to our human limits
as we try to imagine the reign of truth
that you envision for us.

When we follow worldly powers
  and stray from the good path
    you desire for all you have created,
      give us Jesus.
Give us Jesus, O God—
  not a Jesus high and lifted up,
    but chained and arraigned by authorities
      with boldness to tell the truth.
Speak through our words and deeds,
  that your will may be done in our time.
Embolden us with the confidence
  that your reign will one day come.
Come, O Strong One, come. Amen.

Words of Assurance (2 Samuel 23, Revelation 1)
God's promises are everlasting, ordered and secure.
God loves us and frees us.
Accept God's forgiveness, for we are forgiven. Amen.

Response to the Word (2 Samuel 23, John 18, Psalm 132)
Dawn on us, word of truth, like the light of the morning,
like a lamp to light our way.

THANKSGIVING AND COMMUNION

Offering Prayer (Revelation 1)
Abundant God,
  prophecy says you are coming with the clouds
    for every eye to see.
Until that day,
  may the tithes and offerings we bring each week
    do the holy work of making your reign
      real in this community
        and in this world in need. Amen.

SENDING FORTH

Benediction (Revelation 1, John 18)
God calls us into the world
  to embody a realm that is not of this world.

Go forth now in the name of the one who is,
    and was, and is to come.
May God's grace and peace be with you. Amen.

CONTEMPORARY OPTIONS

Contemporary Gathering Words (John 18, Revelation 1)
Let's pause and take a breath.
Between turkey and carols,
   "black Friday" and "cyber Monday,"
   let's pause and take a breath, looking for signs,
   listening for sounds of a realm not of this world.
It's real. It's truth. It's the reign of Christ—
   the reign that was with us before, is with us now,
   and is still not yet fully here.
Let's pause and breathe in life and love and truth.

—OR—

Contemporary Gathering Words (Revelation 1, 2 Samuel 23)
From the Spirit who was, the Rock who is,
   the Strong One yet to come,
   grace and peace to you!
Come before God with joy and thanks.
Let us worship God.

Praise Sentences (John 18, Revelation 1, Psalm 132)
A crown of thorns belongs to the truth.
A crown that gleams belongs to the truth.
The ruler of kings belongs to the truth.
Glory and dominion belong to the truth.
Listen to Jesus. Belong to the truth.

DECEMBER 2, 2012

First Sunday of Advent
Kate Cudlipp

COLOR
Purple

SCRIPTURE READINGS
Jeremiah 33:14-16; Psalm 25:1-10; 1 Thessalonians 3:9-13;
Luke 21:25-36

THEME IDEAS
How can we participate in the coming reign of Christ?
That is the challenge of Advent. God promises a new
order, the birth of a world in which justice and righteousness rule. The promise is irrevocable—the birth will come.
Whether we are among those who will be reborn with that
world depends upon our commitment and allegiance, in
each moment of our lives, to the one true God rather than
the false gods we so often honor. God shows us the way
in the life and words of Jesus, and gives us companions—
our sisters and brothers in Christ. But ultimately, each of
us must actively prepare if we are to be part of what is
being born at Christmas.

INVITATION AND GATHERING

Call to Worship (Jeremiah 33, 1 Thessalonians 3, Luke 21)
People of faith, prepare for the coming reign
of Christ!

As we gather to pray and sing and listen,
a spirit of anticipation and hope fills us.
The days are surely coming, says Our God,
when justice and righteousness will prevail.
May our worship illuminate our hearts
and minds, freeing us to respond joyfully
to God's call in the days to come.

Opening Prayer (Psalm 25, 1 Thessalonians 3, Luke 21)
Holy Source of life and hope,
    as we come together this day,
        open our ears to hear,
        open our eyes to see,
        and open our hearts to love,
            that we may come to know your ways
            and follow your paths.
Help us grow in love for one another,
    and for all creation,
        as we prepare for the coming of the one
            who calls us to turn from our false gods
            to you, Holy One,
                the true source of our salvation. Amen.

PROCLAMATION AND RESPONSE

Prayer of Confession (Jeremiah 33, Luke 21)
Loving Creator, you call us to rejoice
in your promise of the birth that is to come,
but we are afraid.
    You invite us into a world
    where justice and righteousness prevail,
    but we turn away in fear.
We long for an easy path into your promised world,
but you warn us that there is no easy way.
    Birth new life within us, Holy Midwife,
    that we may abide in your perfect love—
    the love that casts out fear.

Words of Assurance (Psalm 25, 1 Thessalonians 3)
God's mercy and steadfast love endure,
  strengthening our hearts and overcoming our fears.
God will remove every obstacle
  that keeps us from being the body of Christ.
  Amen.

Passing the Peace of Christ
Anticipating the blessings of the one who is coming, let
us offer one another signs of Christ's peace:
The peace of Christ be with you, always.
  And also with you.

Response to the Word (Luke 21)
Ever-faithful Teacher of Truth,
  your word is born anew each moment.
It will never pass away.
Grant that we may be bearers of that word,
  bringing your love and hope and justice
  into this violent, hurting world. Amen.

THANKSGIVING AND COMMUNION

Invitation to the Offering (1 Thessalonians)
God's love for us knows no bounds. In grateful response,
may our gifts to others abound.

Offering Prayer (Luke 21)
Giver of all good things,
  as we offer these gifts to you,
  open our eyes to see more clearly
    all that we have been given
    and all that we have to give.
Stretch our capacity to give of ourselves:
  our love, our companionship,
    and our material resources,
      wherever they are needed. Amen.

SENDING FORTH

Benediction (1 Thessalonians 3, Luke 21)
Go into the world awake to the signs
of God's invitations to new life.
Know that the reign of Christ draws nearer
with each right action we choose.
Amen.

CONTEMPORARY OPTIONS

Contemporary Gathering Words (Luke 21)
People of faith, prepare for the coming reign
of Christ!
We are getting ready!

Praise Sentences (Luke 21)
The Chosen One is coming in a cloud
with great power and glory!
Thanks be to God!
The beloved Son is coming in humble estate
with a love that embraces all.
Thanks be to God!

DECEMBER 9, 2012

Second Sunday of Advent

B. J. Beu

COLOR

Purple

SCRIPTURE READINGS

Malachi 3:1-4; Luke 1:68-79; Philippians 1:3-11;
Luke 3:1-6

THEME IDEAS

The message of God's salvation is like a refiner's fire or
fullers' soap—cleansing us of our impurities. While the
advent of the Messiah is marked with hopeful expecta-
tion, preparing for that arrival places demands upon our
lives. With words that confront our complacency, John the
Baptist warns us to repent and amend our lives. Christ is
coming—bringing hope, eagerness, and anticipation, but
also a little fear and trepidation.

INVITATION AND GATHERING

Call to Worship (Malachi 3, Philippians 1)
Prepare the way of the Lord.
Christ comes like a refiner's fire,
burning away the impurities within.
Prepare the way of the Lord.
Christ comes like fullers' soap,
cleansing our sin and purifying our hearts.

Prepare the way of the Lord.
Christ comes like a master gardener,
bearing a harvest of righteousness.

Opening Prayer (Philippians 1, Luke 1, Luke 3)
God of mystery,
  you enter the wilderness of our lives,
    calling us to prepare for Christ's coming.
Fill the valleys of our hearts
  and bring low the mountains
    of our pride and conceit.
Make straight the paths of our feet,
  that we may follow in your ways.
Smooth out the rough edges of our souls—
  edges that chafe those we should hold close—
    and guide our feet in the ways of peace.
As we prepare once more for the advent of your Son,
  keep us in full fellowship with you
    and with one another,
      that our lives may bear a harvest
        of righteousness. Amen.

PROCLAMATION AND RESPONSE

Prayer of Confession (Malachi 3, Luke 1, Luke 3)
Merciful God,
  how quick we are to recognize
    our neighbors' need to amend their ways;
  how easily we spot the speck in their eye,
    ignoring the log in our own.
Come to us like a refiner's fire and fullers' soap,
  that we may be purified in body and soul.
Polish us like fine gold and silver,
  that our ways may be pleasing to you,
    full of compassion and love
      for all we meet. Amen.

Assurance of Pardon (Luke 1)

The One who looked with favor
   upon the descendants of Abraham
   has sent Christ to redeem us from slavery
   to aimlessness and sin.
Through Jesus,
   God's tender mercy dawns from on high,
   bringing light to our darkness
   and life to those who sit in the shadow of death.

Response to the Word (Luke 3:4b-6)

We have heard the good news that salvation is at hand. We have heard the warning to return to God. We have heard the promise of life eternal to those who amend their lives. Let us hear it again, lest we forget: "Prepare the way of the Lord, make his paths straight. Every valley shall be filled, and every mountain and hill shall be made low, and the crooked shall be made straight, and the rough ways made smooth; and all flesh shall see the salvation of God." Amen!

THANKSGIVING AND COMMUNION

Offering Prayer (Malachi 3)

O God, you rescued your people of old,
   you rescue us again and again.
With refiner's fire and fullers' soap,
   you have purified us like works
      of fine gold and silver.
As people brought to the brightness of your dawn,
   may our offerings be pleasing to you, Holy One;
   may they be for the world
      a harvest of righteousness, compassion,
         and love. Amen.

SENDING FORTH

Benediction (Luke 1, Luke 3)

God meets us in the wilderness of our lives,
preparing our hearts to meet the Lord.
   Christ guides our feet in the ways of life.

God fills the valleys of our hearts
and brings low the mountains of our pride.
Christ guides our feet in the ways of love.
God makes straight the paths of our feet
and smoothes out the rough edges of our souls.
Christ guides our feet in the ways of peace.
Go and prepare the way of the Lord.

CONTEMPORARY OPTIONS

Contemporary Gathering Words (Malachi 3, Luke 3)

If your soul feels more tarnished than your jewelry,
take heart.
Our God is like a refiner's fire
and fullers' soap.
If your spirit feels marred by life's difficult choices,
have hope.
Our God will polish us up
brighter than the finest silver and gold.
If your heart feels too beat down to praise God,
be at peace.
Our God breaks into our darkness
filling us with light, love, and joy.
Let us prepare for Christ's birth
and rejoice in the salvation of our God.

Praise Sentences (Luke 3)

Praise the One who brings us the knowledge
of salvation.
Praise the One who shines light in our darkness.
Praise the One who forgives our sins
with compassion and mercy.

DECEMBER 16, 2012

Third Sunday of Advent

B. J. Beu

COLOR

Purple

SCRIPTURE LESSONS

Zephaniah 3:14-20; Isaiah 12:2-6; Philippians 4:4-7;
Luke 3:7-18

THEME IDEAS

With the exception of the Gospel lesson, Philippians cap-
tures the mood of the day: "Rejoice in the Lord always;
again I will say, Rejoice" (v. 4). God's salvation is at hand.
Isaiah and Zephaniah invite us to sing aloud and shout
for joy. Through God, the warrior receives victory while
the lame and outcast no longer live in shame. Three of
today's lections celebrate the joy of our salvation—but the
Gospel lesson reminds us that salvation demands more
than our joy. Beyond calling sinners to repent, John the
Baptist warns of the wrath to come for those who hear the
good news and reject it. Justice is the order of the day. Salvation entails judgment, and we need to be ready.

INVITATION AND GATHERING

Call to Worship (Zephaniah 3, Isaiah 12, Philippians 4:4)
Rejoice in the Lord, always, again I say rejoice!

> With joy, we draw water
> from the well of salvation.
Sing aloud, O daughters of the Holy One.
> With thanks, we return home
> to the living God.
Shout for joy, O sons of the Most High.
> With praise, we approach the throne of grace.
Rejoice in the Lord, always, again I say rejoice!

Opening Prayer (Zephaniah 3, Isaiah 12)
Redeemer God,
> we come to you with laughter in our hearts
> > and joy in our very bones,
> > > for you save the lame
> > > > and take away the shame of the outcast.
When we think all hope is lost,
> you gather us in and bring us home.
Restore our fortunes, O God,
> that we may show everyone we meet
> > your power to transform the world. Amen.

PROCLAMATION AND RESPONSE

Prayer of Confession (Luke 3)
God of justice,
> before we get carried away with our alleluias,
> > remind us once more that salvation may be free,
> > > but it places demands upon us.
How often do we find ourselves
> on the wrong side of your good news?
We forget that the fire of your baptism
> is a purifying fire—
> > a fire consuming those whose spirits
> > > are closed off from the world.
Forgive us when we praise you with our lips
> but curse you with our actions:
> > when we hoard our wealth,
> > when we withhold mercy from the needy,
> > when we cheat the weak and defenseless.

Heal our hearts, Compassionate One,
    that we may be a people of true repentance—
  a people who prepare for your Son's birth
    by embracing those he loved. Amen.

Words of Assurance (Zephaniah 3, Luke 3)

Although the axe is lying at the root of the tree,
    do not despair.
Christ has taken away the judgments against us,
    and invites us even now to embrace
    the joy of our salvation.
Return home to God
    and live as God intends,
    with peace, justice, and great love.

Response to the Word (Luke 3)

John the Baptist preached and baptized to bring us to God. Christ preached and baptized to bring us to God. Let us not shut out the lessons they teach: to love one another, to be a people of justice and mercy, to bring hope in every task we do. Amen.

THANKSGIVING AND COMMUNION

Offering Prayer (Psalm 4)

God of overflowing love and joy,
    you provide all that the world needs—
      but you do not share your gifts around;
      you leave that up to us.
May these offerings be a sign of our willingness
    to be good stewards of your bounty,
      sharing what we have with those in need,
      that we may escape the destruction
        that selfishness brings to our lives.
We pray this in the name of the one
    who embodied selfless giving,
      the one who is to come,
      the one for whom we wait. Amen.

SENDING FORTH

Benediction (Philippians 4)
Rejoice! The Lord is near.
Take heart and do not worry about your life.
And may the peace of God,
that passes all understanding,
guard your hearts and minds in Christ Jesus.

CONTEMPORARY OPTIONS

Contemporary Gathering Words or Benediction (Zephaniah 3, Isaiah 12)
Sing aloud, daughters of the living God.
Shout to the Lord, sons of the God of hosts!
Christ is the fountain of our salvation.
Shout for joy, daughters of the living God.
Sing your praises, sons of the God of hosts!
Christ is the one who leads us home.

Praise Sentences (Zephaniah 3, Philippians 4)
Christ is near.
Rejoice and shout your praise!
Christ is near.
Laugh and sing!
Christ is near.
Alleluia!

DECEMBER 23, 2012

Fourth Sunday of Advent
Mary J. Scifres

COLOR
Purple

SCRIPTURE READINGS
Micah 5:2-5a; Luke 1:46b-55; Hebrews 10:5-10; Luke 1:39-45

THEME IDEAS
The long-awaited promised one comes. Micah prophesies this Shepherd-Ruler will bring security and peace to God's people. Mary sings the ancient song of fortune's reversal when God enters our world with hope for the despairing and humility for the proud. Elizabeth's child leaps in her womb, and Elizabeth proclaims with joy the blessing of Mary's child. The long-awaited promised one comes.

INVITATION AND GATHERING

Call to Worship (Micah 5, Luke 1)
Leap for joy! Christ is coming!
   Christ comes into our lives!
Rejoice and praise! God's promises reign!
   Christ comes into our lives!
Sing songs of old! Proclaim ancient truths!
   Christ comes into our lives!

—*OR*—

Call to Worship (Luke 1)

My soul magnifies the Lord.
My spirit rejoices in God my Savior!
God has looked upon us with smiles of love and joy.
**God has blessed us from generation
to generation.**
Let us worship and praise our great God of mercy.

Opening Prayer (Micah 5, Luke 1)

Blessed God,
   we thank you for blessing us
      with your presence in Christ Jesus
         and your presence in our lives.
With joy,
   we come to worship and praise you,
      as we remember your ancient promises
         now fulfilled.
With anticipation,
   we pray for that day when the truth of your love,
      and the promises of justice and peace,
         will fill every corner of this great earth.
In Christ's name, we pray. Amen.

—*OR*—

Opening Prayer (Micah 5, Luke 1)

Ancient of Days, blessed Child of God,
   be with us this day.
Guide us in your path of peace.
Lead us on the journey of faith
   that will bring us to the joy of Christmas day.
Help us believe where we have not seen,
   that we may trust in your promises,
      like Mary before us.
In your holy name, we pray. Amen.

PROCLAMATION AND RESPONSE

Prayer of Confession (Luke 1)
Magnificent God,
look upon us with your loving favor.
Shine upon us with the light of your wisdom.
Strengthen us in our weakness,
that we may know the power of your love.
Scatter us in our pride,
that we may learn the humility of servanthood.
Forgive us when we weaken others,
and forget your place in our lives.
Lift us up when we are disheartened,
and nourish us with your abundant grace.
Help us, O Promised One of Israel,
to be your people and to serve your world.
Help us live as Advent people:
hopefully expectant, and patiently diligent,
that we may bring your realm to this earth. Amen.

Words of Assurance (Luke 1)
O magnify the Lord! Rejoice in God, our Savior!
For God looks with favor on our lowliness,
lifts us from the depths of sin and despair,
and restores us to fullness of life in Christ Jesus.
Arise, take heart, all are forgiven now!

Passing the Peace of Christ (Luke 1)
Turn to your neighbor and greet one another with signs of
joy and peace!

Response to the Word (Luke 1)
May our souls magnify God with praise
and thanksgiving!
**May our lives reflect God's compassion
and kindness.**
For God has looked gently upon us with mercy
and love.
We are blessed by Christ's amazing grace.

God's strength overcomes our every weakness.
Christ, the bread of life,
fills us with everything we need.
May our lives be life-giving bread for the world.
May our riches become abundance for others.
May God's promises be reflected in our lives,
that we may truly magnify the Lord!

Unison Prayer (Luke 1)

As Christmas comes,
enter our hearts, O God;
make us reflections of your love.
As the hurriedness of the season rushes to meet us,
remind us to enter the homes of loved ones
in anticipation of joy.
In this season of celebration,
help us be signs of celebration for others,
that in us they may find generous friends.
In Christ's name, we pray. Amen.

THANKSGIVING AND COMMUNION

Invitation to the Offering (Luke 1)

Jesus, making himself poor, freely gave God's mercy and
grace. May we scatter seeds of abundance and compassion, as we share the richness of generosity and love to a
world in need.

Offering Prayer (Luke 1)

Mighty God, magnify these gifts,
even as we magnify your name with praise.
May the gifts we give and the lives we lead
be abundant reflections of your glory and love.

SENDING FORTH

Benediction (Luke 1)

As Mary before us, set out with haste
on the journey of life!

We go forth to a world in need.
As Jesus before us, offer hope and love.
We go forth with gracious and generous hearts.
As Elizabeth before us, prepare for good news.
We go forth rejoicing in praise,
for Christ is coming soon!

CONTEMPORARY OPTIONS

Contemporary Gathering Words (Luke 1)

Come, singing of grace.
Come, dancing with joy.
As Mary once sang God's praises,
    so now we are invited to worship and praise
    in honor of Christ.
Let us sing and dance with hope!

Contemporary Gathering Words or Praise Sentences (Luke 1)

Praise to God on high!
We rejoice in God our savior!
Christ looks with favor upon the least and the last.
We rejoice in God our savior!
Our mighty God has done great things for us.
We rejoice in God our savior!
God's mercy is upon those who love.
We rejoice in God our savior!
Christ lifts us out of our despair.
We rejoice in God our savior!
Christ fills our empty souls
and sends away our selfish desires.
We rejoice in God our savior!
God remembers the promises of mercy.
We rejoice in God our savior!

Praise Sentences (Luke 1)

Magnify the Lord, who is worthy to be praised!
Magnify the Lord, who is worthy to be praised!

DECEMBER 24, 2012

Christmas Eve
Laura Jaquith Bartlett

COLOR

White

SCRIPTURE READINGS

Isaiah 9:2-7; Psalm 96; Titus 2:11-14; Luke 2:1-20

THEME IDEAS

The message of God's incarnate love is so powerful in the familiar Luke story that even the once-a-year church folks get it time and time again. We are called to make sure that visitors and regulars alike hear the compelling invitation to live in the light that God has shined into the darkness. This means not just hearing the Christmas story, but telling its good news to others until we ourselves become reflections of Christ's light throughout the year.

INVITATION AND GATHERING

Call to Worship (Isaiah 9, Psalm 96, Luke 2)
The people who walked in darkness
have seen a great light.
   Celebrate the coming of the Light.
O sing to the Lord a new song,
God's salvation is at hand.
   Celebrate the coming of Salvation.

For a child has been born for us, a son given to us.
Celebrate the coming of the Prince of Peace.
I bring you good news of great joy for all the people.
Celebrate the coming of Christ!

Opening Prayer (Isaiah 9)
God of light and love,
    shine upon us this Christmas Eve
        and in the year ahead.
Guide us out of darkness
    and into your joyous light.
May our lives reflect your glorious love,
    that others may see your Christmas Spirit in us,
        each and every day of our lives. Amen.

PROCLAMATION AND RESPONSE

Prayer of Confession (Isaiah 9, Psalm 96, Titus 2, Luke 2)
God of Joy,
    we come to celebrate again
        the arrival of Love Incarnate
            here in our very midst.
Your glorious arrival
    is enough to cause the forests to sing for joy,
    yet we still find reasons to complain and sigh.
Your light of salvation
    is bright enough to illuminate
        every corner of our lives,
        yet we still find ourselves shrouded
            in worry and doubt.
Your gift of Love
    is big enough for the whole world,
    yet we still find ourselves resentful
        that your love extends to those
            whom we deem to be unworthy.
God, you invite us into the light of the stable
    where the overlooked and forgotten have gathered
        to celebrate the miracle of your love.

Give us the strength and courage
    to join you at the manger. Amen.

Words of Assurance (Luke 2)
Do not be afraid!
Hear the good news of great joy for *all* people:
    a savior has been born this night for you!

Passing the Peace of Christ (Luke 2)
As you greet those around you, offer these words:
    "Hear the good news!"
Respond in kind:
    "A Savior is born!"

Prayer of Preparation (Luke 2)
Surprising God,
    open our ears to hear this familiar story
        as if for the first time.
Open our eyes to see the diverse cast
    gathered at the manger.
Open our hearts to the power of your love
    as revealed in this amazing story.
Open our lives to the possibility of transformation,
    as we encounter once again
        God-With-Us, Emmanuel. Amen.

Response to the Word (Isaiah 9, Titus 2, Luke 2)
A child has been born to us.
    Glory to God in the highest heaven!
A savior has been given to us.
    Glory to God in the highest heaven!
The grace of God has appeared in human form.
    Glory to God in the highest heaven!
Salvation has come to all the earth.
    Glory to God in the highest heaven!

THANKSGIVING AND COMMUNION

Invitation to the Offering
(To be spoken by the worship leader, but not printed)
There is a sentiment among some churches that taking an
offering on Christmas Eve is inappropriate. The feeling

goes that it's presumptuous, if not downright rude, for us to expect guests to come to a Christmas celebration and then be asked to put money in the offering plate. But we have a different perspective here. We are so grateful . . . so excited . . . so *changed* by the love that God has shown us in the gift of Jesus Christ, that we simply can't walk away from here without responding. The same God who chose to come to earth as a tiny baby invites us to shine the light of love into the world. Through our gifts this night, we have the opportunity to say thank you; to say yes to life and salvation; to say, "Glory to God in the highest heavens!"

Offering Prayer (Luke 2)
Dear God,
> we cannot thank you enough
> > for the gift of your Son.

Through your grace,
> you have given us everything,
> > including our very lives.

On this night,
> we celebrate the miracle of Christmas!

But when the candles are blown out,
> when the ringing of the bells has ceased
> when the angels and shepherds have gone home,
> may we continue to shine your light into the world
> > through the giving of these offerings.

And so we offer you yet another gift:
> our partnership to build your reign here on earth.
> Amen.

SENDING FORTH

Benediction (Luke 2)
Do not be afraid.
> **We go forth with courage!**

Share the good news.
**We go into the world
to proclaim tidings of great joy!**
A savior has been born to you.
Glory to God in the highest heaven!

CONTEMPORARY OPTIONS

Contemporary Gathering Words (Isaiah 9, Psalm 96)
Sing to the Lord a new song.
Joy to the World!
Tell everyone about God's amazing miracle.
Joy to the World!
A child has been born who is the Prince of Peace.
Joy to the World!
The light of God's love shines
throughout the universe.
Joy to the World!

Praise Sentences (Isaiah 9, Psalm 96)
Hear the good news: a child has been born for us!
He shall be called Wonderful Counselor, Mighty God,
Everlasting Father, Prince of Peace.
He will judge the world with righteousness,
and the peoples with truth.

DECEMBER 30, 2012

First Sunday after Christmas
Mary J. Scifres

COLOR
White

SCRIPTURE READINGS
1 Samuel 2:18-20, 26; Psalm 148; Colossians 3:12-17;
Luke 2:41-52

THEME IDEAS
Spiritual growth into God's ways was obvious in the lives
of Samuel and Jesus. In this letter to the Colossians, we
are all called to grow into God's ways of compassion,
kindness, humility, and patience. Clothed in love and wisdom, Samuel and Jesus served not only God but humanity as well. Clothed in love and wisdom, we are called to
serve God and humanity, as we join the great praise of creation for the One who has created and clothed us with
glory and grace.

INVITATION AND GATHERING

Call to Worship (Colossians 3, Luke 2)
Sing praise to God with gratitude and joy.
    Let heaven and earth praise God!
Dwell in Christ's word of wisdom and truth.
    Praise Christ for the path of life!

Opening Prayer (Colossians 3, Luke 2)
God of wisdom and grace,
    may your Spirit grow within us,
        that we may grow in wisdom and truth
            all the days of our lives.
Teach us your ways,
    that we may walk the path of Christ
        and lead others into your light.
Clothe us with compassion and kindness,
    with humility and gentleness,
    that others may see in us
        the truth of your love.
Bind us together in love and unity,
    that our church may be a haven of blessing
        and a place of peace.

PROCLAMATION AND RESPONSE

Prayer of Confession (Colossians 3, Luke 2)
Merciful Christ,
    you call us to clothe ourselves in love,
        walk in your truth,
            and grow in God's wisdom.
But these garments are often awkward,
    your path sometimes rocky,
        and this growth not always comfortable.
Forgive us when we seek our own comfort
    rather than your more difficult road.
Forgive us when we prefer comfy old shoes
    to the new footwear you offer us
        to follow more challenging paths.
Clothe us in your truth and bind us to your love.
Weave us with the threads of your grace,
    that we may be cloaks of blessing—
        woven in kindness and compassion,
            mercy and patience—
                for those who need protection and love.

Weave us with the threads of your mercy,
   that we may be a community of faith and wisdom,
   reaching out to those who yearn
      to walk in your ways.
In your holy name, we pray. Amen.

Words of Assurance (Luke 2)

Hear the promise of Christmas:
   Christ has come with mercy and grace!
Christ walks with us even now.
   Rejoice, my friends, in Christ we all are forgiven!

Passing the Peace of Christ (Colossians 3)

As God's chosen and beloved, bound in mercy and grace,
let us share signs of peace and love with one another.

Response to the Word or Benediction (Colossians 3)

Called by Christ and beloved by God,
we are called to grow in grace.
   Woven in love and knit together
   with gentleness, we are bound in harmony
   and peace.
Clothed with compassion and fitted with kindness,
we are dressed to show mercy and love.
   We go forth with hope, with gratitude,
   and with joy for this marvelous gift of God!

THANKSGIVING AND COMMUNION

Invitation to the Offering (Colossians 3)

Whatever you do in word or deed, do in the name of
Christ Jesus. Whatever you give in abundance or out of
great poverty, give in the name of Christ Jesus. Let us give
thanks, as we share what we have been given, as signs of
God's love for the world.

Offering Prayer (1 Samuel 2, Colossians 3)

Holy and Beloved One,
   we thank you for the amazing gifts you give to us:

love and kindness, mercy and grace,
abilities and strengths, talents and tools,
even our material wealth.
Receive these gifts we return to you.
Receive our willing hearts,
ready to answer your call
and live in your love.
Bless these gifts,
and bless us as we give of ourselves,
even as you bless those who receive our offering.
In Christ's name, we pray. Amen.

SENDING FORTH

Benediction (Colossians 3, Luke 2)
As God's chosen ones,
go forth with compassion and love.
As holy and beloved ones,
we go into the world with peace.
Woven together in love,
may we be signs of mercy and grace.
With gratitude and joy,
we go forth to love, as Christ loved.

—OR—

Benediction (Colossians 3, Luke 2)
Beloved of God, go forth to love God's world.
Friends of Christ, go forth to befriend others.
Blessed of the Spirit, go forth to be a blessing.
Amen and amen.

CONTEMPORARY OPTIONS

Contemporary Gathering Words (Colossians 3, Luke 2)
Come, clothed in the glory of Christ!
Clothed in what?
Come, clothed in Christian love!
Clothed in what?

Come, clothed in compassion and mercy!
Clothed in what?
Come, clothed in patience and kindness!
Clothed in what?
Come, beloved of God, Christ calls us to live in love.
As we answer that call, the Spirit grows in our lives,
that we may be clothed in glory and love,
compassion and mercy, patience and kindness—
cloaks of protection for a world in need
of God's grace.
Clothed in love, we come!

Praise Sentences (Psalm 148, Colossians 3)
Praise God in heaven and earth!
Praise God in heaven and earth!
Praise God for love and grace!
Praise God for love and grace!

CONTRIBUTORS

Peter Bankson
Peter Bankson is part of the Celebration Circle Mission Group and the Servant Leadership Team of Seekers Church, a Church of the Savior congregation in Washington, D.C.

Laura Jaquith Bartlett
Laura Jaquith Bartlett is an ordained minister of music and worship at a United Methodist retreat center in the foothills of Oregon's Mt. Hood.

B. J. Beu
B. J. Beu is senior pastor of Neighborhood Congregational Church in Laguna Beach, California. A graduate of Boston University and Pacific Lutheran University, Beu loves creative worship, preaching, and advocating for peace and justice.

June Boutwell
June Boutwell is a United Church of Christ pastor currently serving as Executive Director of Pilgrim Pines Camp and Conference Center, located in the Southern California Nevada Conference, UCC.

Mary Petrina Boyd
Mary Petrina Boyd enjoys the opportunities for urban ministry as pastor of University Temple United Methodist Church in Seattle, WA. She loves to weave, spin, and sew, and works on an archaeological dig in Jordan.

Joanne Carlson Brown
Joanne Carlson Brown is the clergy person serving Tibbetts United Methodist Church in Seattle, WA. She is also an

adjunct professor at Seattle University School of Theology and Ministry and lives in Seattle with Thistle, the wee Westie.

Ken Burton
Ken Burton is a member of the Celebration Circle Mission Group of Seekers Church in Washington, D.C.

Kate Cudlipp
Kate Cudlipp is a member of the Servant Leadership Team and the group that writes worship liturgies for Seekers Church in Washington, D.C.

Rebecca J. Kruger Gaudino
Rebecca J. Kruger Gaudino is a United Church of Christ minister in Portland, Oregon, who teaches world religions and biblical studies as Visiting Professor at the University of Portland. She also writes for the United Church of Christ.

Jamie Greening
Jamie Greening is the senior pastor of First Baptist Church, Port Orchard, Washington, where he makes his home with his wife and two daughters. He is also the author of *The Haunting of Pastor Butch Gregory and Other Stories*.

Hans Holznagel
Hans Holznagel has served in communication, mission interpretation, administrative, and fundraising roles in the national ministries of the United Church of Christ since 1984. He and his family live in Cleveland, Ohio, where they are members of Archwood United Church of Christ.

Bill Hoppe
Bill Hoppe is the music coordinator for Bear Creek United Methodist Church in Woodinville, Washington, and is a member of the band BrokenWorks, for which he is the keyboardist. He thanks his family and friends for their continued love, support, and inspiration.

Amy B. Hunter
Amy B. Hunter is a poet and writer, published in *The Christian Century*, and an Episcopal layperson serving in Chelmsford, MA, as an Associate to the Rector for Adult Christian Formation.

Sara Dunning Lambert
Sara Dunning Lambert is mom, wife, nurse, child of God, and worship coordinator at Bear Creek United Methodist Church in Woodinville, Washington.

Sandra Miller
Sandra Miller is a worship leader at Seekers Church in Washington, D.C., where she also serves on the peace and justice mission group called Eyes to See, Ears to Hear. She is also the administrative coordinator at Community Vision, a day program with enriched social services for homeless adults where she teaches a class in expressive writing in addition to her other duties.

Matthew J. Packer
Matthew J. Packer is a music director at the Flushing United Methodist Church in Flushing, Michigan, and an M.Div. student at the Methodist Theological School in Delaware, Ohio.

Mary J. Scifres
Mary J. Scifres serves as a consultant in leadership, church and culture, worship, and evangelism from her Laguna Beach home, where she and her spouse, B. J., reside with their teenage son, Michael. Her books include *The United Methodist Music and Worship Planner, Prepare!* and *Searching for Seekers*.

Deborah Sokolove
Deborah Sokolove is the director of the Henry Luce III Center for the Arts and Religion and associate professor of Art and Worship at Wesley Theological Seminary, and is part

of the group that writes liturgy for Seekers Church, an ecumenical Christian community in Washington, D.C.

Leigh Anne Taylor
Leigh Anne Taylor is the minister of music at Blacksburg United Methodist Church and lives with her family in the mountains of southwest Virginia.

SCRIPTURE INDEX

(Page numbers in italics refer to the CD-ROM.)

SCRIPTURE INDEX

SCRIPTURE INDEX

COMMUNION LITURGIES INDEX

In order of appearance

SONG AND HYMN INDEX

BAPTISMAL RESOURCES

In order of appearance

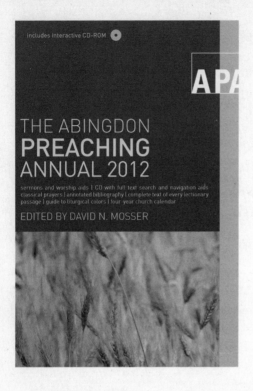

Preachers have long turned to *The Abingdon Preaching Annual* for help with the central task of their ministry: sermon preparation. The 2012 edition of the *Annual* continues this fine tradition with lectionary-based and topical sermons for flexibility in choice, additional lectionary commentary, and worship aids for every sermon. The CD-ROM, included with every book, provides classical and contemporary affirmations and prayers, plus hyperlinked planning aids such as bibliographical references, and the full lectionary texts for each Sunday. *The Abingdon Preaching Annual* is now one of the most comprehensive and useful resources for sermon preparation that you will find on the market.

"Commendations to Abingdon Press for offering two fresh ecumenical resources for pastors."

For *The Abingdon Preaching Annual*—"Anyone who dares proclaim a holy word week in and week out soon realizes that creative inspiration for toe-shaking sermons quickly wanes. Multitasking pastors who are wise seek out resources that multiply their own inductive initiatives."

For *The Abingdon Worship Annual*—"Not only the sermon but also the whole service dares to be toe-shaking . . . and the *Worship Annual* is a reservoir of resources in that direction."

—The Reverend Willard E. Roth, Academy of Parish Clergy President, *Sharing the Practice: The Journal of the Academy of Parish Clergy*

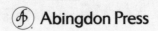
Abingdon Press

DO YOU HAVE THE BOOK YOU NEED?

We want you to have the best planner, designed to meet your specific needs. How do you know if you have the right resource? Simply complete this one-question quiz:

DO YOU LEAD WORSHIP IN A UNITED METHODIST CONGREGATION?

YES.

Use *The United Methodist Music and Worship Planner, 2011 -2012*
(ISBN: 9781426710179)

NO.

Use *Prepare! A Weekly Worship Planbook for Pastors and Musicians, 2011 -2012*
(ISBN: 9781426710162)

To order these resources, call Cokesbury Music Service toll-free at 1-877-877-8674, visit your local Cokesbury store, or shop online at www.cokesbury.com. Do you find yourself rushing at the last minute to order your new planner? Subscribe today and receive your new *The United Methodist Music and Worship Planner* or *Prepare!* automatically next year and every year. Call toll-free 1-800-672-1789 to request subscription.